Maye Clar

Marge Clark

Christmas Thyme
at
Oak Hill Farm

Photograph by Richard Clark

Marge Clark

Christmas Thyme
at
Oak Hill Farm

Holiday Parties *Homemade Gifts*
Holiday Decorations

Photography by Bill Hopkins
Cover photography by Bill Hopkins
Food styling by Judy Vance and Patti Florez
Book design by Mauck+Associates/Angie Hoogensen

Publisher
Thyme Cookbooks
Marge Clark
Oak Hill Farm
6242 West State Road 28
West Lebanon, IN 47991-8054

Other Books by Marge Clark:

Take a Little Thyme by Marge Clark and Ann S. Harrison
It's About Thyme! by Marge Clark

Published by Thyme Cookbooks, Marge Clark,
Oak Hill Farm, 6242 West State Road 28, West Lebanon, IN 47991-8054

Library of Congress Catalogue Card Number
94-90065

Clark, Marge
Christmas Thyme at Oak Hill Farm
Index Included
1. Menus - Recipes   2. Holiday Decorations   3. Homemade Gifts

ISBN 0-9640514-5-1

Second Printing

Printed by
RR Donnelley & Sons Company

*This book
is dedicated to the
memory of my Mother
and Father. They taught
me what Christmas is
really about.*

Acknowledgments

There are so many friends to thank for helping make this book a reality. Naomi Freeman, Freeman's Folly Antiques Shop, Rossville, Illinois • Crystal Luttrell, Williamsport, Indiana • Juanita Bannon, The Weed Patch, West Lebanon, Indiana • Bill and Nancy Pearson, Attica Floral, Attica, Indiana • Arnet Davis, Davis Flowers, Williamsport, Indiana • Molly Culbert, Flowers and Gifts by Molly, Hoopeston, Illinois • Bob and Bonnie Wright, The Beef House Restaurant, Covington, Indiana • Mae DeBord, West Lebanon, Indiana • Rusty and Ann Harrison, Attica, Indiana • Joy Mabry, Paquet Farms, Slidell, Louisiana • Mirsky's, Beaverton, Oregon • Helen Harriman, Buffalo, New York • Don Haynie and Tom Hamlin, Buffalo Springs Herb Farm, Raphine, Virginia • Berry's Garden Center, Danville, Illinois • Cynthia Marie Clark, Williamsport, Indiana • Tom Bookwalter, Perrysville, Indiana • Shirley Kerkhove, Attica, Indiana • Virgil Scowden Antiques, Williamsport, Indiana

Special thanks to three special and talented people. Nancy Clark, who is "word perfect" on her computer! Nancy prepared all the copy and disks for the graphics people. She always knew just how I wanted it done — since I don't talk "computer language," that probably wasn't easy for her to figure out just what I did want.

Cynthia Bookwalter, who gave untold hours helping set up for the gift section photography. I'm not sure it would have gotten done without her — I do know for sure the pictures are great because of her help.

Carl Taylor, who came after his regular job hours to help with trees and wreaths in those hectic days preparing for photography.

And then of course, special thanks to Bill Hopkins, photographer extraordinaire, whose pictures grace some of the pages of magazines you probably have on your coffee table.

If you think the food you see on the menu pages looks "good enough to eat," it's because of two talented food stylists — Judy Vance and Patti Florez.

And to the creative talents of Kent Mauck and his graphic associates who designed each page of the book, thank you.

Last, but certainly not least, thanks to my husband, Dick, who took the picture of the house (it was zero that day!). He is my constant source of encouragement, whatever I do.

Contents

Introduction

Oak Hill Farm has been home to my husband, Dick, me, and our four sons for many years. Some of our out-of-the-area friends ask if ours is a "working" farm, or just a place in the country. Well, it is certainly a "working" farm! Besides field crops we grow on the farm, we have always had large vegetable and flower gardens. Because of our interest and love of gardening, it only seemed natural to add an herb garden, and so in the last several years, the herb garden has also become a part of our "working" farm. Of the gardening we do, it is perhaps the most enjoyable. I know of nothing more rewarding than walking through an herb garden on a beautiful summer day, being surrounded with the most wonderful aromas imaginable.

This book is a story about how we celebrate Christmas at Oak Hill Farm and on these pages you'll soon learn how the herb garden and its harvest plays a big role at Christmastime. Herbal gifts of vinegars, oils, butters, potpourris and more are included on these pages as well as instructions on how to make an herbal advent wreath, a rosemary wreath, lemon verbena potpourri and much more. But this is a book anyone can use — there are menu and recipe ideas, gift suggestions and many decorating ideas besides the herbal ones I mentioned. Hopefully, you'll see some ideas and recipes on these pages that you can use. At any rate, this is the way Christmas at Oak Hill Farm is celebrated.

When the boys were all home, we used to decorate seven trees in the house — three downstairs and a small one in each of the four bedrooms upstairs. Now, we decorate the three downstairs, starting the day after Thanksgiving with our goal of finishing **all** decorating by the end of the first week of December. That gives us two weeks to entertain, leaving the last week for family activities.

We usually have the four parties discussed in the book — Come For Coffee, A Buffet for Friends, A Christmas Tea, and Christmas Eve at Oak Hill Farm — and the parties are in that order! The food I talk about on these pages, the decorations, the traditions — this is truly the way we celebrate Christmas. Many of the recipes are old family ones that have been used for years at Holiday time. Many decorations are several years old and are stored each January so they can be brought out in late November to be "hung with care" again.

For a long time, family and friends have urged me to tell this Christmas story, and so here is *Christmas Thyme at Oak Hill Farm*. A story about the "most wonderful thyme of the year"!

Marge Clark
Oak Hill Farm
Winter - 1994

Christmas
Thyme Parties

Come for Coffee

A morning get-together with good friends is a wonderful way to relax and listen to everyone tell about their Christmas plans! It's the type of party where the guests may hurry in for a cup of coffee, a piece of delicious coffee cake, tell us how busy they are, and rush out to tackle more shopping, cooking or decorating. It's also the type of party where your guests may arrive at nine and leave at noon with apparently all shopping and Christmas chores completed. Best of all, it's a party where guests are urged to come casual, sit down by the fire and simply unwind. Who of us doesn't need to be invited to at least one of these parties during the Holidays?

The food I serve at such a get-together must be relatively easy to prepare, made ahead of time and, if possible, frozen until ready to use. There must also be a minimum of preparation time on the morning of the party.

With this menu, remove your frozen cakes, etc., from the freezer the night before. In the morning, unwrap and arrange your baked things, mix the fruit, turn on the coffee pot and light the fire in the fireplace. Sit down with the first cup of coffee and wait for the doorbell to ring. You and your friends are going to have a glorious morning! The food isn't bad either . . . .

Come for Coffee Menu

Ann Greenfield's Christmas Coffee Cake

Raspberry Cream Cheese Coffee Cake

Italian Sweet Bread
(Pandolce)

Butter

Winter Ambrosia
with Sour Cream and Honey Dressing

Coffee
Sugar — Cream

Ann Greenfield's Christmas Coffee Cake

This is a variation of the sour cream and streusel coffee cake we all know and love. The addition of sliced apples makes the cake moist and delicious. I receive many recipes in the mail from people who have purchased one of my books and want to share a favorite recipe. We can all thank Ann Greenfield for sending me this recipe!

1	cup pecans, chopped
1½	cups sugar, divided
1	teaspoon ground cinnamon
2	cups flour
1	teaspoon baking powder
1	teaspoon baking soda
½	teaspoon salt
½	cup butter or margarine
2	large eggs
1	teaspoon vanilla
1	cup sour cream
1	large cooking apple (I like Red or Yellow Delicious), peeled and sliced

Grease a 9" tube pan. Combine pecans, ½ cup sugar and the cinnamon in a small bowl. Set aside. In a medium bowl, combine flour, baking powder, baking soda and salt. In a large mixer bowl, combine the shortening and the remaining 1 cup of sugar. Beat until creamy. Add eggs and vanilla and beat until light and fluffy. Add flour mixture alternately with the sour cream, one quarter at a time, beating well after each addition. Peel and slice the apple.

Heat oven to 325°. Spread half of the batter in bottom of prepared pan. Arrange apple slices on batter and sprinkle half the pecan-sugar mixture on the apples. Add remaining batter and sprinkle remainder of pecan-sugar mixture on top. Bake 50 to 60 minutes, or until a pick comes out clean. Check after 50 minutes. Remove from oven and cool in pan for 15 minutes. Invert pan onto serving plate. When cake is out of pan, carefully turn cake upright. Serve as is, or drizzle a little confectioners' sugar icing over top and let it drip down the sides. If desired, wrap the cooled cake well and freeze for up to one month before using it. If you freeze cake, wait until serving time to drizzle on the icing. Cake will serve 12 to 15. It is superb.

Raspberry Cream Cheese Coffee Cake

Probably one of the best coffee cakes I ever ate! Very rich and absolutely wonderful.

2½	cups flour
1	cup sugar, divided
¾	cup margarine
½	teaspoon baking powder
½	teaspoon baking soda
¼	teaspoon salt
¾	cup sour cream
1	teaspoon almond extract
1	egg
1	8 ounce package cream cheese, softened
1	egg
½	cup best quality red raspberry preserves
½	cup sliced almonds

Preheat oven to 350°. Grease and flour a 9" or 10" springform pan with a solid bottom (not a tube pan). In a large bowl, combine flour and ¾ cup sugar. Cut margarine into flour mixture with a pastry blender to make coarse crumbs. Reserve 1 cup of this crumb mixture. To remaining crumb mixture, add baking powder, baking soda, salt, sour cream, almond extract and 1 egg. Blend well. Batter will be stiff. Spread batter over bottom and 2" up sides of the prepared pan. Batter should be about ¼" thick on sides. In a small bowl, combine cream cheese, ¼ cup sugar and 1 egg. Blend well. Pour into batter-lined pan. Carefully spoon preserves evenly over cheese mixture. In another small bowl, combine the reserved 1 cup crumb mixture and the almonds. Sprinkle over preserves. Bake for 45 to 55 minutes, or until cream cheese is set and crust is golden brown. Check after 45 minutes. Cool 15 minutes. Carefully remove sides of pan. Let cake cool completely while it's still on the springform pan bottom. When cool, run knife around bottom of pan (between the cake and the pan) to loosen the cake. Place cake on serving plate. If you wish to freeze the cake, wrap it well and freeze up to 2 weeks. Thaw, wrapped, when ready to serve. Refrigerate any leftover cake. Very rich, so cut into small servings. Will serve 16 to 20.

Italian Sweet Bread

If you choose one bread to make for your coffee party, this is the one. I have made this several times at Holiday time and it never fails to be a big hit. It is moist, sweet and full of wonderful things. This recipe is from an old Italian friend. She says that in Italy, this bread is called pandolce, which means "sweet bread."

1³/₄	cups milk
³/₄	cup sugar
1	teaspoon salt
¹/₂	cup butter or margarine
³/₄	cup warm water (105° to 115°)
2	packages active dry yeast
7	cups all-purpose flour, unsifted
2	teaspoons fennel seed
1	teaspoon anise seed
1¹/₂	cups golden raisins
¹/₃	cup pine nuts (if you can't find these, substitute walnuts)
¹/₂	cup shelled pistachio nuts, chopped
¹/₂	cup candied lemon peel, chopped
¹/₂	cup candied citron, chopped
3	tablespoons grated orange peel
3	tablespoons Marsala* wine
1	egg yolk
2	tablespoons water

In a small saucepan, heat milk until bubbles form around edge of pan. Remove from heat. Add sugar, salt and butter. Stir until butter is melted and sugar is dissolved. Cool to lukewarm. Combine yeast with the warm water; check water temperature with thermometer to be sure it's in the 105° to 115° range. (This, by the way, is very important to remember in all your yeast baking. Water too hot will kill the yeast action, and if it's too cool, the yeast won't be active enough.) Gently stir the yeast into the water until yeast is dissolved. Stir in the lukewarm milk mixture and mix well. Add 4 cups flour and beat until smooth, 2 minutes or so. Gradually add rest of flour and beat another 2 minutes. With your hands, mix until dough leaves side of bowl. Turn mass out onto a floured surface and knead for 5 minutes. Grease a large bowl. Shape dough into a ball and put into the bowl. Cover with a piece of lightly greased waxed paper. Then cover with a clean dish towel. Set bowl in a warm draft-free place and let rise for about 1 hour, or until doubled in bulk. While dough is rising, prepare other ingredients. Spread the fennel and anise seeds on a bread board; roll and crush seeds with a rolling pin. In a medium bowl, combine raisins, nuts, fennel and anise seeds, lemon peel, citron, orange peel and Marsala. Mix well. Let stand.

Now, turn dough out onto a floured surface and roll to a 14" x 14" square about ¹/₂" thick. Sprinkle surface with the fruit mixture. Roll up, jelly-roll style. Use your rolling pin and reroll to a 13", or so, square. Cut in half and shape each half into rounds on a large, greased cookie sheet. Cover with a clean towel and let rise in a warm place for about 1 hour, or until doubled. Preheat oven to 350°. With scissors, make 3 cuts in top of dough to form a triangle. Brush with the egg yolk beaten with water. Bake about 1 hour, or until golden brown. Cool completely. If desired, wrap, label and freeze for up to 1 month. Makes 2 simply wonderful loaves of bread.

* Marsala wine is the principal dessert wine of Italy. It is made in northwest Sicily. It is dark red and has the taste of burnt sugar. It is matured in wooden casks for 2 to 5 years before it's bottled. If you can't find Marsala, substitute the best sherry you can find.

Winter Ambrosia with Sour Cream and Honey Dressing

Combine **fresh orange sections, fresh grapefruit sections, sweetened coconut** (from a can), and **pomegranate seeds** in a large bowl. The amount you prepare depends on the number of guests you expect. Fresh pineapple pieces are also a good addition.

For the dressing, combine ½ **cup sour cream, 1 tablespoon honey, 1 tablespoon orange juice,** and **2 tablespoons Grand Marnier, Cointreau,** or any other orange-flavored liqueur. Or, omit the liqueur and use 2 more tablespoons of orange juice. Carefully mix dressing into the fruits. This amount of dressing will dress fruit for about 8 servings. Serve in Christmas printed plastic or paper cups, if desired.

To save time the morning of the party, I prepare my orange and grapefruit sections the day before, place them in zip-type plastic bags and refrigerate. The day of the party, drain off juice that may have accumulated in the plastic bags. Use that juice in the dressing recipe. The dressing is best made at the time you'll be using it.

A Christmas Buffet for Friends

A buffet is a marvelous way to entertain. Food and drink are arranged on a serving table or sideboard and guests help themselves. This Christmas Buffet is planned for 12 people. I've chosen a favorite casserole our friends like at Holiday time. It is definitely a do-ahead meal that requires very little last minute preparation.

Since there are two kinds of punch, set up a table for the two bowls. Place a bowl on either end of the table. The punches are both red, so they look especially pretty on a crisp white tablecloth. Surround each punch bowl with a simple evergreen wreath. Decorate each wreath with Christmas-red bows. Nestle some pine cones, small apples, kumquats, walnuts, or other fruits, nuts, even flowers, into the greenery. There is an ice ring recipe for the Cranberry Vodka Holiday Punch. For the Spiced Fruit Punch, freeze orange slices or other fruits in an ice ring. If your punch table is large enough, gather several candles (choose different sizes, shapes, heights, etc.) and arrange on the table. At party time, light the candles. Arrange punch cups near each bowl and let your guests help themselves. Pass the appetizers or ask a friend to help with that chore.

A stack of plates, the main dish
(Turkey Tetrazzini in this case), the salad and
a basket of muffins all go on the serving table or
the buffet. If there isn't room on this table for flowers
or a Christmas arrangement, make room for at least one or
two candles to light. Candles and a little greenery will make the
buffet festive indeed.

When everyone has finished eating, clear the tables and the serving table
and set the buffet with dessert, dessert plates, forks, spoons, etc. If there's
room on the buffet, place the dessert on one end and coffee, cups and saucers
on the other end.

After dessert and coffee, it's nice to offer an array of after-dinner liqueurs,
but of course, this is optional.

The secrets to a successful buffet-type party are few, but oh so important.
Make the food preparation easy; make the serving easy; make clean-up quick
and easy. The whole idea is for you to enjoy the party as much as your
guests do! This is a great way for you to relax with friends during
the hectic days of preparing for the Holidays. I'm quite sure you
will find the food every bit as delicious and festive as roast
turkey and all the trimmings, but a whole lot easier!

Do plan a Christmas Buffet — you and
your guests will love it!

Christmas Buffet for Friends Menu

Serves 12 people

Cranberry Vodka Holiday Punch

Spiced Fruit Punch

Chili Cheese Squares

Salted Nuts

Cheese Board and Crackers

Turkey Tetrazzini

Cinnamon Candied Apples or Pears

Green Salad with Mandarin Oranges and
Water Chestnuts with Orange Walnut Vinaigrette

Cranberry Orange Honey Nut Muffins

Poppy Seed Yogurt Muffins

Butter

Annie's Apple Pudding

Coffee
Sugar - Cream

A Tray of After-Dinner Liqueurs

Cranberry Vodka Holiday Punch

Serving a punch for a Holiday party is certainly easier than offering a variety of drinks. Let everyone help themselves to a cup of this beautiful and delicious drink.

1	12 ounce can frozen orange juice concentrate, thawed
3	cups water
1/2	cup orange liqueur (Grand Marnier, Cointreau, Triple Sec, etc.)
2	quarts cranberry juice cocktail
1	fifth vodka
1	32 ounce bottle lemon-lime carbonated drink

Combine the orange juice concentrate, the water and the orange liqueur and pour into a ring mold. Freeze to make an ice ring (make sure this ring will fit into your punch bowl!). At serving time, combine cranberry juice cocktail, vodka and the lemon-lime drink in a large punch bowl. Add ice ring and serve. This gets better and better as the ice ring melts! Makes about 20 punch cup servings.

Spiced Fruit Punch

This is a non-alcoholic punch. It's spicy and very good.

1	cup water
1/4	cup sugar
3	cinnamon sticks
1	teaspoon whole cloves
2	cups cranberry juice cocktail
1 1/2	cups pineapple juice
1	quart ginger ale

Combine water, sugar and spices in a small saucepan. Bring to a boil and boil gently for 5 minutes. Remove from heat and let mixture cool to room temperature. Strain and discard the spices. Add the cranberry juice cocktail and pineapple juice. Stir well. Pour mixture into a punch bowl. At serving time, add the ginger ale. Stir gently. Add ice ring and serve. Makes 8 cups. Recipe can easily be doubled or tripled.

Green Salad with Mandarin Oranges and Water Chestnuts with Orange Walnut Vinaigrette

Choose an assortment of lettuces. Clean them several hours before the party and store clean, dry leaves in plastic bags in the refrigerator. Make the vinaigrette ahead of time also. This is just the right sweet and tangy flavor to serve with the tetrazzini. It is a fabulous vinaigrette.

12	cups assorted greens (good choices are butter, Bibb, Boston, leaf and iceberg)
2	cups canned mandarin orange slices, drained
1	cup water chestnuts, sliced
1½	cups vegetable oil
⅓	cup walnut oil*
3	teaspoons Dijon mustard
	grated zest of 2 oranges
3	tablespoons orange juice
3	tablespoons balsamic vinegar*
3	tablespoons sherry vinegar*
1½	teaspoons soy sauce
½	teaspoon salt
¼	teaspoon pepper
½	cup toasted walnut pieces, optional

Prepare greens, bag and refrigerate. Whisk together the oils, mustard, zest, juice, vinegars, soy sauce, salt and pepper in a medium bowl. Transfer vinaigrette to a covered jar and refrigerate. At serving time, place greens in a large bowl. Add mandarin orange slices, water chestnuts and toasted walnuts; toss to distribute. Add vinaigrette and toss well to coat leaves. Serve immediately. Makes 12 servings.

* Walnut oil, balsamic vinegar and sherry vinegar are all available from specialty or gourmet food stores, or watch some of the catalogs, such as Williams-Sonoma, for these items. This vinaigrette is excellent mainly because of these 3 special ingredients.

Turkey Tetrazzini

Here is a wonderful recipe you'll be happy to add to your files. It is a perfect one-dish meal for your Holiday Buffet. This recipe will serve 12.

1	16 ounce package spaghetti
1	tablespoon butter
1½	sticks butter, divided
1	medium onion, diced
½	pound fresh mushrooms, cleaned and sliced
½	cup flour
6	cups milk
3	teaspoons chicken-flavored instant bouillon granules
1	teaspoon salt
½	cup grated Parmesan cheese
1	10 ounce package frozen peas, unthawed
1	4 ounce jar diced pimento
3	tablespoons fresh parsley, chopped
8	slices firm white bread
6	to 8 cups cooked turkey breast, cut into small cubes or pieces

Cook spaghetti in a large saucepan according to label directions. Drain. Return spaghetti to the pot. Add the 1 tablespoon of butter and toss to coat strands of spaghetti so they don't stick together. Cover pot and set aside.

Melt 6 tablespoons of butter in a large saucepan. Cook onion over medium heat until tender. Add mushrooms and cook and stir for 3 or 4 minutes. With a slotted spoon, remove the mushrooms and onions to a bowl. (You may need to add a tablespoon or two of butter to the saucepan at this point.) Stir flour into pan and blend into the butter mixture. Gradually stir in the milk, bouillon and salt. Cook, stirring until mixture is smooth and slightly thickened. Remove from heat. Stir in the cheese, mushrooms and separated frozen peas. Add diced pimento and chopped parsley and mix gently, but thoroughly. Taste and add salt and pepper if needed.

Place the bread slices in a food processor. Process on/off to make soft bread crumbs. Do not overprocess. In a saucepan, melt the other 6 tablespoons of butter. Remove from heat. Toss bread crumbs into the melted butter.

Add the sauce mixture and the cubed turkey to spaghetti in the large saucepan. Gently toss to mix well. Grease 2 - 9" x 13" baking dishes. Evenly divide the mixture between the 2 dishes. Sprinkle the buttered crumbs over tops of both dishes. If serving now, place the baking dishes in a preheated 350° oven for about 30 minutes, or until hot and bubbly. You may make the tetrazzini the day before serving, if desired. If so, cover dishes and refrigerate. Bring to room temperature before baking.

I cook one whole turkey breast for this recipe.

Cinnamon Candied Apples

I like this recipe so much, you'll also find it in the other two books I've written. Sometimes I call this recipe Cinnamon Jonathans because the best apples to use are Jonathans. I have made these apples at Christmas time for the last 20 years! By the way, you can substitute small, firm, peeled pears for the apples. Sometimes I do some of each. These are incredibly beautiful in a footed glass or crystal compote.

1	cup sugar
2	cups water
1	cup cinnamon red hot candies
	small, firm apples, such as Jonathans

Combine the sugar, water and red hots in a fairly large, deep saucepot. Bring to a boil and simmer until red hots are dissolved and thoroughly melted. Peel small, firm apples. Drop apples into the boiling syrup — keep syrup boiling, so just add 3 or 4 apples at a time. Cook until apples (or pears) are just tender, but not mushy. This is enough syrup to cook 6 or 8 apples, so for a party for 12, double the recipe.

Chili Cheese Squares

This great recipe comes from Jeanette Groves and Cynthia Bookwalter — mother and daughter in that order! They are both fabulous cooks and when they suggest I try a recipe, I try it — I can count on it being a good one.

Prepare this dish early in the day. Cover and refrigerate. Bake about an hour before guests are due.

8	eggs
1/2	cup flour
1	teaspoon baking powder
3/4	teaspoon salt
3	cups shredded Monterey Jack cheese
1 1/2	cups cottage cheese
2	4 ounce cans green chilies, drained, seeded and chopped

Beat eggs until light — 3 to 5 minutes. Stir together the flour, baking powder and salt. Add dry ingredients to the egg mixture and mix well. Fold in cheeses and chopped chilies. Grease a 9" x 9" x 2" pan. Add filling to pan and bake in a 350° oven for about 40 minutes. Remove pan from oven and let set for 10 minutes. Cut into small cubes to serve. Makes about 3 dozen squares.

Cranberry Orange Honey Nut Muffins

There aren't enough superlatives to describe these muffins. They are moist, not too sweet and full of wonderful flavors we associate with the Holidays. Each recipe makes 18 muffins.

2	cups unbleached flour
1	cup bran
2	tablespoons baking powder
2	eggs, lightly beaten
1	cup water
$\frac{1}{2}$	cup honey
$\frac{1}{2}$	cup butter, melted
1	large, seedless navel orange
$1\frac{1}{2}$	cups fresh cranberries, picked over and washed
$\frac{1}{2}$	cup chopped pecans or walnuts

Combine flour, bran and baking powder in a large bowl. Stir in eggs, water, honey and melted butter. Cut the orange into pieces, including the rind, and place in a food processor or blender. Process to a mush. Chop cranberries coarsely. Now add the orange mixture, the chopped cranberries and the nuts to the batter and stir just until combined. Do not over-mix. Fill greased muffin tins almost level. Bake in a preheated 400° oven for 20 minutes, or until baked through.

If you like a tangy, cranberry-orange muffin, then you'll like these. They are definitely not sweet, so the fruit flavors are very predominant. I guess I'm trying to tell you that I really like these muffins!

Poppy Seed Yogurt Muffins

Another great muffin — moist, dense and sweeter than the Cranberry Orange Honey Nut Muffins. Equally as good, though. This recipe makes about 12 delicious muffins.

2	cups all-purpose flour
3	teaspoons poppy seeds
$\frac{1}{2}$	teaspoon salt
$\frac{1}{4}$	teaspoon baking soda
1	cup sugar
$\frac{1}{2}$	cup butter, softened
2	eggs
1	cup plain yogurt
1	teaspoon vanilla

Combine flour, poppy seeds, salt and baking soda in a small bowl. In a large bowl, cream together the sugar and the butter. Beat in eggs, one at a time. Blend in yogurt and vanilla. Add the flour mixture and stir until ingredients are thoroughly moistened. Fill greased muffin pans $\frac{2}{3}$ full and bake in a 400° oven for 15 to 20 minutes, or until a wooden pick comes out clean.

Annie's Apple Pudding

Annie's Apple Pudding

Annie is a good friend who doesn't mind sharing good recipes with me! This fabulous pudding is similar to the date pudding that makes that wonderful sauce as it bakes. It's very rich, so one 9" x 13" pan will probably be enough for 12 people. It doesn't take long to put this together and I think the pudding is best if made the day it's served. Serve with a bowl of whipped cream nearby, if desired (this is totally optional as it's already outrageously rich!).

1	to 1⅓ cups sugar (depends on tartness of apples)
⅔	cup shortening
2	eggs, beaten
6	cups apples, peeled and chopped
2	teaspoons baking soda
2	teaspoons ground cinnamon
1	teaspoon ground nutmeg
2	cups flour
1	cup chopped pecans or walnuts

Cream sugar and shortening. Add eggs, one at a time, and beat well after each addition. Fold in the chopped apples and the nuts. Sift together the baking soda, spices and flour and add to the apple mixture. Spread the apple mixture into a greased 9" x 13" pan and pour the following sauce over the top.

Sauce

1½	cups brown sugar, packed
2	tablespoons flour
1	cup water
¼	cup butter
1	teaspoon vanilla

Stir together the brown sugar and the flour, then add remainder of ingredients in a heavy saucepan. Bring to a boil and boil gently for 3 minutes, stirring often. Pour this hot sauce over the batter. Do not stir. Bake at 325° for 1 hour.

A Christmas Tea

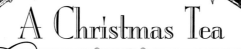

Of the entertaining we do at Christmas time, this party is the "fanciest" of them all. I bring out the best linen and lace tablecloth, crystal and silver and put a spectacular centerpiece on the table! (It is usually a topiary of beautiful fruits with flowers and fresh rosemary in water tubes added for beauty and fragrance.) Most of the baking for this tea is done in advance and kept frozen until party time. I do like to make the scones fresh, though, the morning of the tea. I make the tea sandwich fillings the day before and also make the nesselrode custard the day before.

On the day of the tea, I arrange all the baked goods on serving plates or cake stands — remove the wrappings at the last minute to keep everything fresh. I'll fill the phyllo nests at the very last minute and assemble the tea sandwiches late in the morning. Cover the trays with clean tea towels to keep sandwiches from drying out. It will now take only a few minutes just before the party to get everything on the table. Once it's on the table and the guests have arrived, about the only thing to do is keep the cookie tray filled and make sure the tea and coffee pots are full.

Tea should be served from 4 o'clock to 6 o'clock, but sometimes for convenience I'll make the hours from 3 o'clock to 5 o'clock. I think we need to set the time to suit the occasion and the guests and don't worry too much about what is the "right" time. This is the one daytime party where it's perfectly admissible to light all the candles in the house — and I do! So, turn on the Christmas music, light the fireplace and enjoy your "shining" party.

Christmas Tea Menu

Scotch Scones with Dried Cranberries
Orange Butter
Devon or Pretend Clotted Cream
Strawberry Jam

Lemon Cream Loaves

Brandied Apricot Teacakes

Don Haynie's Rose Geranium Cake

Light Fruitcake

Dark Fruitcake

Phyllo Nests with Nesselrode Filling

Fabulous Pecan Bars

Viennese Pastry Envelopes

Candy Canes

Coconut Snowdrops

Tea Sandwiches

Candied Rose Petals

Hot Spiced Cranberry Tea

Coffee
Sugar - Cream

Scotch Scones with Dried Cranberries

At Holiday time, it's nice to substitute dried cranberry bits for the raisins. If you're near a specialty or gourmet food shop, do splurge on the real Devon clotted cream to serve with these scones. Once a year, it's worth every calorie! Traditionally, you must serve strawberry jam with the scones..

2	cups flour
½	cup raisins or currants or dried cranberries (if cranberries are large, cut each in half or quarters)
2	tablespoons sugar
3	teaspoons baking powder
1	teaspoon salt
¼	teaspoon baking soda
½	cup sour cream
¼	cup vegetable oil
3	tablespoons milk
1	egg, slightly beaten

Heat oven to 425°. Combine the first 6 ingredients in a large bowl. Add remainder of ingredients and stir until dough holds together. On a well-floured surface, roll the ball of dough until it is no longer sticky. Knead dough 12 or 15 times. Divide ball in half. Pat each half into a 6" circle. Brush surfaces with a little milk, then sprinkle a little sugar on each. Cut each circle into 8 wedges. Place 2" apart on a very lightly greased cookie sheet. Bake for 10 to 12 minutes. Serve hot, if possible, with butter, a flavored butter, honey, or jam and of course, clotted cream. Each recipe makes 16 scones, so you may need to make more than 1 batch for your tea. They are best warm, but if that's not possible, cool them after they're baked, then wrap well and serve at room temperature — and serve them the same day they're baked.

Orange Butter

This is an excellent flavored butter to serve with the scones. Offer this butter as a substitute for the strawberry preserves and the clotted cream.

1	cup butter, softened
2	tablespoons orange marmalade

Mix together thoroughly and serve at room temperature. Try this on biscuits, toast, English muffins, or waffles.

Pretend Clotted Cream

If you can't find the real thing, this is a fairly good substitute, but I have to tell you, nothing really takes the place of Devon cream. This rich and thick cream comes from the Devonshire, England, area. You've probably heard that compared to France, Italy and other European countries, the food in England is rather bland. That may or may not be true of other parts, but it certainly isn't true of Devonshire. We have had wonderful food in inns and small hotels throughout this region. Naturally, Devon cream is widely used, especially in desserts. I'll never forget a bowl of fresh strawberries and Devon cream served outside on the terrace of a small country inn....

  4   ounces whipped cream cheese (you can buy it this way in a small round tub)
  ¹/₂   cup unsalted butter, softened

Beat the cream cheese and butter together in a small bowl until very well mixed. Cover and refrigerate until serving time.

Viennese Pastry Envelopes

Serve these delicate little pastries warm, whether straight from the oven or rewarmed in a low oven. They are very easy to make and literally melt in your mouth.

  6   ounces unsalted butter, softened
  6   ounces cream cheese, softened
  2   egg yolks (if eggs are small, use 3 yolks)
1¹/₃ cups flour
      whole strawberry jam
      confectioners' sugar

Mix the first 4 ingredients together in a medium bowl to form a soft dough. Turn dough onto a floured surface and roll into a sheet ¹/₄" thick. Cut into 2" squares. Place ¹/₂ teaspoon of jam in the center of each square. Fold the 4 corners toward the center, pressing edges together as firmly as possible. It helps to keep fingertips floured. Place on an ungreased baking sheet and bake in a 325° oven about 15 minutes, or until pastry is golden brown — may take a few minutes less or a few minutes more. Watch closely. Dust with confectioners' sugar while cookies are still warm. Makes about 3¹/₂ dozen pastries.

    I usually make these little pastries a few days ahead of when I need them. Wrap unbaked pastries and freeze. On the day of the party, remove from the freezer and let thaw, still wrapped. Remove wrappings and proceed with baking instructions above.

Lemon Cream Loaves

This recipe makes two perfectly wonderful loaves of tea bread. The cream cheese makes the bread moist and rather dense. The lemon verbena is optional, but really adds a lot of "lemony" flavor. Be sure to dry some leaves for winter use.

$\frac{1}{2}$	cup finely chopped pecans or black walnuts (I always use the walnuts if I have them)
1	tablespoon grated lemon rind
1	tablespoon flour
$\frac{1}{2}$	cup margarine
1	8 ounce package cream cheese, softened
$1\frac{1}{3}$	cups sugar
2	eggs
$2\frac{1}{2}$	cups flour
1	tablespoon baking powder
1	teaspoon salt
1	cup milk
1	teaspoon dried, chopped lemon verbena leaves, optional
	Lemon Glaze (recipe follows)

In a small bowl, dredge pecans and lemon rind in 1 tablespoon of flour. Butter two $8\frac{1}{2}$" x $4\frac{1}{2}$" loaf pans. Heat oven to 350°, or 325° if using glass pans. Cream margarine and cream cheese together in a large mixing bowl. Gradually add sugar, beating constantly. Add eggs, one at a time, beating well after each addition. Combine flour, baking powder and salt. Add to creamed mixture alternately with milk, beginning and ending with flour. Mix well after each addition. Stir in nuts, lemon rind and lemon verbena. Divide batter between the 2 prepared pans. Move oven rack to middle of oven and bake for 1 hour or until a wooden pick inserted in the center comes out clean. Make the following glaze a few minutes before cake comes out of oven.

Lemon Glaze

1	tablespoon grated lemon rind*
$\frac{1}{4}$	cup fresh lemon juice
$\frac{1}{4}$	cup sugar

Combine the ingredients in a small bowl. Stir to dissolve sugar as well as possible. Makes about $\frac{1}{4}$ cup.

Brush the glaze over hot loaves. Use all the glaze. Cool in pans for 20 minutes. Remove loaves from pans and cool completely. Wrap in plastic wrap to store, or wrap well and place in freezer up to 1 month before you use them. Like most fruit quick breads, this bread is best if made a day or two ahead of using.

To serve the bread, slice thinly. If desired, spread each slice with a little whipped cream cheese, or a little softened butter.

* When a recipe calls for grated rind — lemon, orange, etc. — be sure to grate only the colored part. The white part of the rind is bitter and will interfere with the clean citrus taste of the rind.

Brandied Apricot Teacakes

I clipped this recipe from a magazine a few years ago and have made it for the tea table ever since. The teacakes are spicy and aromatic, but best of all, delicious. Start this recipe early in the day.

1	6 ounce package dried apricots, finely chopped
1/2	cup currants
1/2	cup boiling water
1/2	cup butter or margarine, softened
1 1/2	cups light brown sugar, firmly packed
3	eggs
2	cups flour
1/2	teaspoon baking soda
1/2	teaspoon salt
1	teaspoon ground allspice
1	teaspoon ground cinnamon
1/2	teaspoon ground cloves
1	cup apricot-flavored brandy
	confectioners' sugar

Combine apricots and currants in a small bowl. Add boiling water. Cover bowl and let stand for 6 to 8 hours. Beat butter and gradually add the brown sugar. Beat well at medium speed with electric mixer. Add eggs, 1 at a time, beating well after each addition. Combine flour and the next 5 ingredients. Add to creamed mixture alternately with the brandy, beginning and ending with the flour mixture. Mix well after each addition. Stir in the fruit mixture.

Spoon batter into paper-lined miniature muffin pans, filling each cup 3/4 full. Bake at 325° for 25 to 30 minutes. Remove the muffins from the pans and let them cool. Sprinkle a little confectioners' sugar over each muffin. Makes 6 dozen little cakes.

These, too, can be wrapped well and frozen. Thaw at serving time. If you freeze them, sprinkle the confectioners' sugar on at serving time.

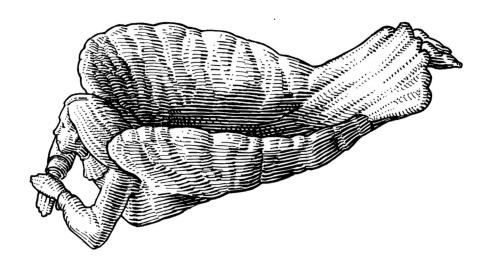

Coconut Snowdrops

Actually, these snowdrops are rich chocolate candies. They look pretty on the cookie tray, though. Remember this recipe for gift giving also — someone would love a box of these.

2 cups confectioners' sugar, sifted
1 cup unsweetened cocoa
²/₃ cup plus 1 tablespoon sweetened condensed milk (not evaporated)
2 teaspoons vanilla
3 cups flaked coconut

Sift confectioners' sugar, then resift sugar with the cocoa into a medium-sized bowl. Make a well in the center and add the condensed milk and vanilla. Stir until well mixed. Mixture will be very stiff and crumbly. Stir in 1 cup of the coconut. Shape into 1" balls* and roll in remaining 2 cups of coconut. Store in an airtight container. May be refrigerated up to 3 or 4 weeks. Makes about 40 to 50 snowdrops.

* Shape the mixture in the palm of your hand. The heat from the palm will aid in shaping the balls.

Dark Fruitcake and Light Fruitcake

Light Fruitcake

This recipe is for all of you who do not like fruitcake! It has wonderful things like light raisins, orange juice, pecans and coconut in it. No heavy glaceéd fruit, but a mellow and moist cake that (almost!) everyone will like.

The women in my church make about 300 pounds of this cake each fall for a fund raiser. Many of our customers tell us they never liked fruitcake until they tasted this one. If you live near my hometown, do buy the cakes from us! If you don't, here is my recipe....

2	cups sugar
1	cup butter
4	eggs
½	cup buttermilk
1	teaspoon baking soda
3½	cups flour
2	tablespoons grated orange peel
1	cup grated coconut
1	cup golden raisins
1	cup coarsely chopped dates
1	cup coarsely chopped pecans

Preheat oven to 300°. Grease and flour a 10" tube pan, or 4 small (1 pound each) loaf pans. Line bottom of pan (or pans) with waxed paper. Grease paper. Cream sugar and butter. Add eggs, one at a time, and beat well after each addition. Combine soda and buttermilk. Add buttermilk alternately with flour. Mix well. Add orange peel, coconut, raisins, dates and pecans. Spoon into prepared pan. Bake the 1 pound loaf pans for 1 to 1¼ hours or until they test done.

A tube pan will take 1¼ to 1½ hours, or more. If the cake appears to be browning too much on top, lay a piece of foil over the cake the last few minutes of baking. When done, remove cake from the oven. Cool cake slightly. Carefully turn cake (or cakes) out of pan and peel off waxed paper. Put cake back into pan and carefully poke holes all over top of the cake — I use a sharp wooden skewer. Drizzle the following glaze on the cake.

Glaze

Dissolve ⅓ **cup sugar** in the **juice of 1 orange**. Heat to a boil and simmer a minute or two. Remove from heat. Add **1 tablespoon grated orange peel**. Drizzle the glaze on — let soak in, and drizzle more on. Use as much of the glaze as the cake will absorb.

Dark Fruitcake

I've had this cake recipe for years. If you like a heavy, spicy, full-of-fruit-and-nuts cake, then you'll like this cake.

The women in my church make about 300 pounds of this cake, as well as the light one previously mentioned. Both light and dark cakes are a must at our house for Christmas, and especially a must for my Christmas tea.

3	cups chopped nuts (I usually use half walnuts and half pecans)
2	cups chopped dates
1	cup candied cherries, cut in half
1	cup candied pineapple
2	cups flour, sifted
1	teaspoon salt
1	teaspoon baking powder
1	teaspoon ground allspice
$^1/_2$	teaspoon ground nutmeg
$^1/_2$	teaspoon ground cloves
1	cup shortening
$^1/_2$	cup sugar
$^1/_2$	cup honey
5	eggs
$^1/_3$	cup orange juice
$1^1/_2$	cups raisins
1	$3^1/_2$ ounce can coconut

Put nuts, dates and candied fruit in a paper bag with $^1/_4$ cup of the flour. Shake to coat well. Turn out into a very large bowl. Sift rest of flour, salt, baking powder and spices. Cream together the shortening and sugar. Stir in the honey. Beat in eggs, one at a time. Beat well after each addition. Add dry ingredients to creamed mixture alternately with orange juice. Beat well. Add raisins and coconut. Pour batter over candied fruit mixture. Mix well with a heavy wooden spoon. Pour into 3 medium loaf pans (greased and floured), or 6 small loaf pans, or 1 large tube pan.

Bake at 275° for $1^1/_2$ to 2 hours (less for the little pans). You may choose to soak cheesecloth in wine or brandy and wrap cooled cakes in this cloth. Wrap cake in cloth, then in plastic wrap or foil to make airtight. Store in refrigerator for at least 2 weeks. Unwrap loaves and brush tops with warm corn syrup. Decorate with candied fruits and nuts. Brush decoration with corn syrup also. Makes approximately 6 pounds of wonderful dark fruitcake.

Phyllo Nests with Nesselrode Filling

These are a bit tedious, but worth every bit of the effort. They make a great show on the tea table. The nesselrode filling I use is a vanilla pie-type filling with bits of glaceéd fruit added. Do not add the filling until the very last minute so the nests retain their crispness. The day before you work with the dough, remove the box from the freezer and place the unopened box in the refrigerator. One box of frozen phyllo dough contains about 20 sheets of dough. Most frozen phyllo sheets are 14" x 18." For this recipe, you need four sheets of dough for six nests, so one box of dough will make 30 nests. These nests fit inside the cups of regular-sized muffin pans. Cut the dough like this:

```
              |— 6" —|
        ┌─────┬─────┬─────┐
        │  1  │  2  │  3  │  7"   (Each nest of 4 is 6" x 7")
  14"   ├─────┼─────┼─────┤
        │  4  │  5  │  6  │       4 sheets of phyllo dough
        └─────┴─────┴─────┘
        |——————— 18" ——————|
```

Stack **4 sheets of phyllo dough** on top of each other. Keep all dough covered with a barely damp tea towel to keep the fragile sheets from drying out. Work quickly and with a sharp knife, cut into 6 pieces (see diagram). Carefully brush each piece with **melted butter**. Butter 4 pieces at a time. Carefully fit each stack of 4 pieces into a greased muffin cup, and with your fingers, gently form into the cup shape. When muffin pan is filled, bake in a 375° oven for 10 to 12 minutes, or until crisp and light brown. Cool, and again, carefully remove the nests from the pan. Store the nests in an airtight container until ready to use. Best if baked the day you use them, but I have made them the day before and they're okay.

Nesselrode Filling

Make this filling the day before the party. Fill the phyllo nests the day of the party. One recipe makes two cups of filling.

³/₄	cup sugar
¹/₃	cup flour
2	cups milk
3	egg yolks, slightly beaten
1¹/₂	tablespoons butter or margarine
1	teaspoon vanilla
¹/₂	cup glaceéd fruit, cut into bits
	whipped cream for garnish, optional
	glaceéd cherry halves for garnish, optional

Mix sugar and flour thoroughly. Add milk gradually. Add slightly beaten egg yolks and blend well with a whisk. Place mixture in a heavy medium-sized saucepan and cook and stir until thickened. Remove from heat and add butter and vanilla. Stir in fruit bits. Cover and cool. When ready to serve, spoon a heaping tablespoon of filling into each phyllo nest. Garnish with a teaspoon of whipped cream and top the cream with a cherry half.

Fabulous Pecan Bars

If I publish 15 books in my lifetime, this recipe will be in all 15! That's how good it is. I tried to give it a new name for this book, but I really couldn't come up with a better one. Don't just make these cookies for the tea table — wherever and whenever you want to serve (or give) about the best cookie ever, do consider this recipe.

Crust

½	cup cold butter
1½	cups flour
¼	cup ice water

Filling

1½	cups light brown sugar, packed
1	cup butter
½	cup honey
⅓	cup sugar
1	pound pecans, chopped (but not too fine)
¼	cup whipping cream

Use a pastry blender to cut butter into the flour. Mixture should resemble cornmeal. Add water and toss with a fork. Gather dough into a ball. Wrap in plastic wrap and refrigerate for 1 or 2 hours. Butter and flour a 9" x 13" pan. Roll dough out to about an 11" x 15" rectangle. Fit dough into the prepared pan and let it come up about 1" on all sides. Pierce dough with a fork. Chill while making the filling. Preheat oven to 400°. Combine brown sugar, butter, honey and sugar in a heavy saucepan and bring to a boil over medium heat, stirring constantly. Boil until thick and dark, 3 or 4 minutes. You must stir constantly. Remove from heat. Stir in pecans and whipping cream. Pour over dough in pan. Bake for about 25 minutes. Check after about 15 minutes. If the filling is browning too much, reduce oven heat to 375° and continue baking. Cool cookies in the pan. Cut into strips. Makes 5 or 6 dozen strips, depending on how large you cut them. Almost better than pecan pie!

Candy Canes

These beautiful twisted cookies are as good as they look! If there are any left, be sure to put them on the cookie tray for Christmas Eve or Christmas Day dinner. The children love them.

¹/₂	cup butter or margarine, softened
¹/₂	cup shortening (I use Crisco)
1	cup confectioners' sugar
1	egg
1	teaspoon vanilla
³/₄	teaspoon peppermint extract (clear, not green or red)
2¹/₂	cups unsifted flour
¹/₂	teaspoon salt
¹/₂	teaspoon red food coloring

Topping

¹/₂	cup finely crushed red and white peppermint candy
¹/₄	cup sugar
1	egg white, slightly beaten

In a large bowl of an electric mixer, combine butter, shortening, sugar and egg. Beat at medium speed until light and fluffy. Add extracts. In another bowl, combine flour and salt. Gradually add flour to creamed mixture and continue beating just until combined. Divide dough in half. Add food coloring to one half and mix color into dough thoroughly. Wrap each half in plastic wrap and refrigerate for an hour.

Preheat oven to 350°. Grease cookie sheets. Pull off about 1 teaspoonful of each dough. On a lightly floured surface, roll each piece into a 5" long rope, using your palms to roll the pieces. Lay the 2 pieces side by side and twist them together. Form into a candy cane shape. Carefully transfer each cane to the cookie sheet. Fill the sheet and bake 10 to 12 minutes or until golden at the edges.

Meanwhile, combine the crushed candy and sugar. When cookies come out of the oven and while they're still on the cookie sheet, brush each lightly with egg white and sprinkle on a little candy-sugar mixture. Remove canes to a wire rack and cool thoroughly. Makes about 3 dozen candy canes. These may be made in advance and frozen for up to one month.

Note: You may make the cookies without the candy-sugar topping, if desired. Just sprinkle a little sugar over tops of the warm cookies. They're good either way.

Don Haynie's Rose Geranium Cake

Don Haynie and Tom Hamlin own a most wonderful farm near Raphine, Virginia, called Buffalo Springs Herb Farm. They serve this special cake to friends and guests who visit the farm to take one of Don's classes or attend their herbal events. Don is charming, witty and most clever with the fresh flower and herb bouquets that he creates.

In order to make this special cake at Christmas time, I gather a few nice rose geranium leaves late in the summer, wash and dry them, wrap each one separately and store them in the freezer until cake-baking time. Remove them from the freezer just a few minutes before putting them in the pan. Of course, if you make this cake in the summer, use fresh leaves.

1	cup butter or margarine
2½	cups sugar
6	eggs, beaten
3	cups flour
½	teaspoon salt
¼	teaspoon baking soda
1	cup sour cream
2	teaspoons vanilla
2	tablespoons rosewater (available at many herb shops or specialty food shops)
¼	teaspoon ground mace
5	or 6 rose geranium leaves

Have butter and eggs at room temperature. Preheat oven to 350°. Blend butter and sugar, then beat until light and fluffy. Add beaten eggs and beat well. Blend dry ingredients together and add alternately with the sour cream to the egg mixture. Add flavorings. Mix well.

If rose geranium leaves are frozen, remove them from freezer at this time. Grease and flour a 9" or 10" tube pan. Spray the rose geranium leaves lightly with nonstick cooking oil and arrange thawed leaves in the bottom of the pan, dull side of the leaves up. Spoon batter into the pan, being careful to not dislodge the leaves. Bake for 1 hour and 10 to 20 minutes, or until a cake tester comes out clean. Be careful not to overbake. After 1 hour of baking, place a piece of foil over top of the cake.

Cool cake in pan for 15 to 20 minutes. Carefully remove cake to serving plate or cake stand. Beautiful and delicious.

I like to drizzle a little confectioners' sugar icing on top and down sides of this cake. Use about **1 cup of sifted confectioners' sugar, 1 teaspoon of rosewater,** and thin with **water** to proper consistency.

Variation: Sometimes Don dries the rose geranium leaves and places them in a zip-lock bag to store. When he needs them for the cake, he chops enough leaves to make 2 tablespoons. He then stirs these pieces into the batter.

Tea Sandwiches

Here are three excellent tea sandwich spreads. The first two can be made in advance and refrigerated until tea time. The cucumber sandwiches should be made just before serving.

I like to use a firm, rather dense bread for these sandwiches (thin-sliced Pepperidge Farm is a good choice). White, wheat, oatmeal, etc., are all good choices.

1. Smoked Salmon with Dilled Cream Cheese

1	8 ounce package cream cheese, softened
$^1\!/_2$	cup smoked salmon, cut into bits
$^1\!/_2$	to 1 teaspoon dried dill weed
	milk for thinning

Combine all ingredients using the milk to thin mixture to spreading consistency. Store in a covered container in the refrigerator until ready to use. Makes about $1^1\!/_4$ cups.

2. Chicken Pineapple Pecan Spread

1	cup cooked, finely chopped chicken
$^1\!/_3$	cup well-drained crushed pineapple
$^1\!/_4$	cup finely chopped pecans
	mayonnaise to moisten
	salt and pepper to taste

Combine all ingredients with enough mayonnaise to make a good spreading consistency. Store in a covered container in the refrigerator until ready to use. Makes about $1^1\!/_4$ cups.

3. English Cucumber Sandwiches

wafer thin slices of unpeeled cucumber
softened butter
fresh parsley

Spread softened butter on small pieces of bread (crusts removed). Lay 2 or 3 thin slices of cucumber on buttered bread. Garnish each with a tiny piece of fresh parsley.

To make all the sandwiches, cut the firm bread into small squares, triangles, rounds, etc. Remove crusts first with a sharp knife. Serve these tea sandwiches open-faced.

Candied Rose Petals

What a beautiful addition to the table! If you've eaten candied violets, then you're ready for candied rose petals. They are sweet and crunchy and probably should be served next to candies or other sweets. Use the darkest red rose you can find for this recipe. Each rose will make 15 or 20 candied petals.

> 1   dark red rose, just ready to come into full bloom
> 2   egg whites
>   sugar (superfine sugar works the best)

Carefully pull all petals off the rose. If necessary, wash and wipe each petal dry. In a small bowl, beat egg whites with a wire whisk until frothy. Place sugar in another small bowl. Take one petal at a time and dip it into the egg white, covering all surfaces. Gently dip into the sugar and "toss" sugar all over petal to coat both sides. Place on a foil-lined cookie sheet. Sprinkle any uncoated areas with sugar. Let dry at room temperature for 2 hours. Turn petals over onto dry foil and let that side dry at least 2 hours. If not thoroughly dry and crystallized, let dry another hour or two, or however long it takes. Gently place in airtight containers with waxed paper between layers. Store in a cool, dry place.

Hot Spiced Cranberry Tea

Each recipe makes 12 cups of beautiful and delicious tea. Many guests will definitely ask for seconds. Serve this tea from the teapot with a pot of coffee next to it.

> 12   cups water
> 12   whole allspice
> 2   small cinnamon sticks
> 1   teaspoon whole cloves
> 12   tea bags or 5 tablespoons loose tea (I like orange pekoe)
> 1   cup light brown sugar, firmly packed
> 1   cup cranberry juice
> $\frac{1}{2}$ cup orange juice
> $\frac{1}{4}$ cup lemon juice

Combine water, allspice, cinnamon sticks and cloves in a medium saucepan. Bring contents to a full rolling boil. Remove from heat and add tea. Cover and steep for 5 minutes. Stir and strain into a large container. Strain again, this time with a coffee filter fitted into the wire strainer — this will make the tea more clear. Add sugar and stir until dissolved. Tea may be made to this point and set aside until serving time. Stir in cranberry juice and the orange and lemon juices. Pour mixture into a large pot or kettle and gently reheat to serve, but **do not boil**.

Christmas Eve at Oak Hill Farm

Christmas Eve is pure excitement for young and old alike! Christmas Eve is for family, for good food, for opening presents, and most of all, to welcome the birth of a baby who would be called Jesus.

A menu for Christmas Eve must include foods that all ages will enjoy. The meal also needs to be relatively easy to put on the table and easy to clean up when it's over. Anything that can be prepared a day or more ahead is surely a welcome choice.

Every year, we, like many of you, wonder if we should have dinner first or presents first. We usually decide on dinner first (even though the children and grandchildren can hardly stand it!), because they can play with new gifts and toys while we "older" ones trudge back to the kitchen to clean it all up. The evening still has plenty of time for another cup of coffee, for visiting and perhaps trying out a new game. Then it's off to church for midnight services lest we forget what the entire season is about!

From all of us at Oak Hill Farm, Merry Christmas!

Christmas Eve at Oak Hill Farm Menu

Cranberry Champagne Cocktail

Mugs of Orange Juice with Cinnamon Stick Stirrers

Pat Reppert's Hot Crab Puffs with Chives

Apricot Baked Ham

Stuffed Baked Potatoes

Green Salad with Herb Dressing

Ruby Red Raspberry Salad

Old Fashioned Ice Box Rolls
Butter - Strawberry Jam

Easy Herbed Bread Sticks

Holiday Cheesecake

Pecan Pie

Frozen Peanut Butter Cups

Gingerbread Boys*

Coffee
Sugar - Cream

Recipe on page 66

Cranberry Champagne Cocktail

This is the easiest and most festive drink I can think of for a Christmas Eve celebration. Offer the children orange juice or cranberry juice cocktail in a mug with a cinnamon stick stirrer.

4 cups cranberry juice cocktail, chilled
1 750 ml. bottle champagne or Asti spumante, chilled

Combine cranberry juice and champagne in a 2 quart pitcher. Stir until blended. Serve chilled. Makes about nine 6 ounce servings.

Pat Reppert's Hot Crab Puffs with Chives

I met Pat through International Herb Growers and Marketers Association. She has an herb business (Shale Hill Farm) near Saugerties, NY. Thanks, Pat, for this excellent hot appetizer recipe.

1 loaf Veri-Thin Pepperidge Farm white bread
1 6½ ounce can lump crab meat, drain and cover with 1 tablespoon lemon juice
½ cup mayonnaise
⅓ cup minced onion
⅓ cup freshly grated Parmesan cheese
1 tablespoon chopped chives or chopped dillweed, or 1 teaspoon dried
1 tablespoon chopped fresh parsley
   dash of salt and pepper

Cut the crusts off the bread. Pick over the crab meat and drain off lemon juice. Mix remainder of ingredients together and stir in crab meat. Spread the slices of bread with the crab mixture. Cut each slice into quarters. Place on a foil-lined tray and bake now in a 425° oven for 10 to 12 minutes, or freeze, uncovered. When thoroughly frozen, remove squares from the tray and place them in zip-type plastic bags and return them to the freezer. When ready to use, spray a foil-lined cookie sheet with a nonstick cooking spray. Place squares on the sheet and bake in a preheated 425° oven for 10 to 12 minutes, or until lightly browned. Makes 4 dozen squares.

Apricot Baked Ham

Ham is a great choice for this meal, because once it goes in the oven, it practically takes care of itself until dinnertime. The best reason I have for serving it is because everyone in my family loves it! The sugary crust makes the ham beautiful to serve.

1	10 to 14 pound whole ham, fully cooked, bone-in
	whole cloves
1/3	cup dry mustard
1	cup apricot jam
1	cup light brown sugar, firmly packed

Trim skin and excess fat from ham. Place ham on a rack in a large roasting pan. Insert cloves in ham every inch or so. Be sure to push cloves into the ham surface as far as they'll go. Now combine the dry mustard and the jam. Spread over entire surface of the ham. Pat the brown sugar over the jam mixture. Bake uncovered, at 325° for 2½ to 3½ hours, or until meat thermometer registers 140°. Count on 15 to 18 minutes per pound. The sugary crust that forms on the ham keeps the juices in. When ham is done, remove it from oven and let ham set for 15 or 20 minutes before carving it. Will serve 15 or more.

Stuffed Baked Potatoes

Everyone loves these stuffed potatoes. I prepare the potatoes up to a week before our dinner, wrap them well and freeze them. Thaw potatoes (still wrapped) the day you wish to bake them. Everyone at our table, from the youngest grandchild and up, loves these potatoes! The recipe serves 6. You can double or more the ingredients for a larger crowd.

3	large baking potatoes (oblong in shape)
1	stick butter, divided
$\frac{1}{2}$	cup half and half cream
$\frac{1}{2}$	cup sour cream
1	teaspoon salt
$\frac{1}{2}$	teaspoon white pepper, or black if white is unavailable
$\frac{1}{2}$	cup green onions, chopped
1	cup grated sharp Cheddar cheese
	butter to melt
	paprika for garnish

Scrub potatoes. Rub skins with vegetable oil. Place potatoes in a shallow pan. Bake in a 400° oven for about an hour. Set aside to cool enough to handle. Carefully cut potatoes in half lengthwise. Scoop out potato pulp into a large bowl — be careful not to damage the shells. Melt one half stick of butter and sauté green onions. To the potato pulp, add other half of butter, the half and half cream, sour cream, salt, pepper, the sautéed onions and the Cheddar cheese. Whip the mixture with electric mixer until smooth. If mixture is too dry, add a bit more cream or sour cream. Stuff the potato shell halves with the mixture. At this point, wrap potatoes and freeze, if desired. When ready to use, thaw potatoes. Melt 4 or 5 teaspoons butter and drizzle a little over each potato. Sprinkle with paprika. Bake in a 350° oven for 30 minutes, or until potatoes are heated through.

Easy Herbed Bread Sticks

Nothing could be easier than this! The ice box rolls are light and tender. By contrast, these rolls are crunchy and crisp. Put some of each in the bread basket.

8	hot dog buns
$\frac{1}{2}$	cup butter, softened
1	tablespoon crumbled rosemary
1	tablespoon sesame seeds
2	tablespoons grated Parmesan cheese

Split buns lengthwise. Cut each half again lengthwise — you now have 4 narrow strips from each bun. Spread each strip with softened butter. Combine rosemary, sesame seeds and Parmesan cheese. Sprinkle evenly over bread sticks. Spray a baking sheet with nonstick cooking spray. Place bread sticks on the sheet and bake at 250° for 30 minutes, or until crisp. Cool. Store in a covered container. Makes 32 bread sticks. They are great!

Green Salad with Herb Dressing

We often have two salads for this meal — a green salad for adults and a gelatin salad for the children. Use this great dressing recipe next time you make a pasta salad.

	assorted salad greens
$1/2$	cup extra virgin olive oil
3	tablespoons fresh lemon juice
3	tablespoons balsamic vinegar*
2	heaping teaspoons Dijon mustard
$1/2$	teaspoon minced garlic
2	teaspoons dried oregano
$1/4$	teaspoon freshly ground black pepper
$1/2$	cup toasted pine nuts, pecans or walnuts**

Clean and dry greens and store in a plastic bag in refrigerator until serving time. Combine all dressing ingredients in a small deep bowl and whisk until well blended. Dress greens, add toasted nuts and serve immediately. This is enough dressing for 12 cups of salad greens. Make a double recipe if in doubt. Leftover dressing is wonderful to have in the refrigerator.

* *Balsamic vinegar is a dark, aged and delicious vinegar from Italy. It is only made in the provinces of Modena and Reggio Emilia. This is a perfectly wonderful area of Italy to visit. Not only is the area home to balsamic vinegar, it is also home of prosciutto ham and the* **real** *Parmesan cheese — Parmigiano-Reggiano.*

** *Place nuts in a small, heavy skillet. Toast over low heat, shaking pan often, for 4 or 5 minutes.*

Ruby Red Raspberry Salad

A beautiful salad to serve. Place a square on a lettuce leaf and garnish.

1	3 ounce package red raspberry gelatin
1	cup boiling water
1	10 ounce package frozen red raspberries, undrained
$1^{1}/2$	cups sour cream
1	3 ounce package cherry gelatin
1	cup boiling water
1	20 ounce can crushed pineapple, drained
1	pound can whole cranberry sauce, or cranberry-raspberry sauce
	mayonnaise for garnish
	mint leaves for garnish, optional

Dissolve raspberry gelatin in hot water. Add red raspberries to gelatin and stir until berries are separated. Place in a 9" x 13" pan. Refrigerate to set. Spread the sour cream over surface of the raspberry layer. Now dissolve cherry gelatin in hot water. Add the crushed pineapple and the cranberry sauce and stir to mix well. Let this mixture cool to room temperature, then spoon it over the sour cream layer. Cover and refrigerate until serving time. Cut into squares to serve. Put a teaspoon of mayonnaise on each square and stick a mint leaf in the mayonnaise, if desired. Serves 12 to 14.

Old Fashioned Ice Box Rolls

This old recipe came from Mother's collection. She always thought Crisco made such light, fine-grained rolls. I have doubled her recipe which will make about 6 dozen rolls. Keep any unbaked dough in refrigerator to bake another day.

1	cup Crisco shortening
3/4	cup sugar
1	cup boiling water
2	packages of active dry yeast dissolved in 1 cup warm water
2	eggs, beaten
1	teaspoon salt
6	to 6½ cups flour (I like bread flour)
	melted butter

Cream Crisco and sugar together well. Add the boiling water and stir to combine thoroughly. Cool mixture to lukewarm and add yeast (that was dissolved in the cup of warm water), eggs and salt. Stir in enough flour to make a soft dough. Knead 2 or 3 minutes on a floured board.

Grease a large bowl. Place ball of dough in bowl and turn to grease all sides. Cover and place bowl in the refrigerator overnight. When ready to use, make rolls into desired shapes. Dip each roll in melted butter. Place rolls in a greased pan. Let rise 1 to 2 hours. Bake at 400° for 15 to 20 minutes.

Frozen Peanut Butter Cups

I make these fabulous little desserts in mini muffin pans. They are rich, delicious and addictive. Again, this is a great recipe for this meal. It must be prepared and frozen several hours ahead, or overnight. It you use the mini muffin pans, recipe will make 24 cups.

1	cup whipping cream
1	7 to 7½ ounce jar marshmallow creme
1	3 ounce package cream cheese, softened
½	cup chunky peanut butter

In a small bowl, with mixer at medium speed, beat whipping cream until stiff peaks form. In a large bowl, with the same beaters and with mixer now at low speed, beat marshmallow creme, cream cheese and peanut butter until smooth. Use a rubber spatula and fold whipped cream into the peanut butter mixture.

Line each mini muffin pan cup with fluted paper or foil baking cups. Spoon the mousse mixture into the cups. Set uncovered pans in the freezer for 15 to 20 minutes (set your timer). Remove pans, wrap well, and immediately place back in freezer. Remove from freezer a few minutes before serving time.

These are wonderful to serve as a light dessert for a luncheon. One or two per serving with coffee is a perfect ending to a Holiday (or any day!) luncheon.

Holiday Cheesecake

This is a fabulous cheesecake with a gingery crust. Another great choice for this Christmas Eve dinner because the cake is best if prepared a day before serving.

1	pound box gingersnaps, finely ground
1/2	cup unsalted butter, melted
6	large eggs
3	cups sugar
1	teaspoon vanilla
1	teaspoon fresh lemon juice
3	pounds cream cheese, softened
3/4	cup raisins (I use light raisins)
1/4	cup light rum
1/4	cup warm water
1	teaspoon grated lemon zest (no white)
1	cup whipping cream
1/2	cup flour
1/2	cup light brown sugar, firmly packed
1/4	cup unsalted butter, chilled and cut into bits

Combine the ground gingersnaps and the melted butter and press mixture on the bottom and up the side of a 10" springform pan. In the large bowl of your electric mixer, beat together the eggs, 2 cups of the sugar, then add vanilla, lemon juice and the cream cheese, and beat until mixture is smooth. Pour mixture into crust in the pan. Bake at 350° for 1 1/4 hours. Turn off the oven and let cheesecake stand in the oven with the door ajar for 1 hour. This will, or should, eliminate the possibility of the cake cracking.

While cake is standing in the oven, put raisins in a small bowl. Add the rum and 1/4 cup warm water. Let raisins soak for about 10 minutes, then drain them. In a saucepan, combine the drained raisins, zest, remaining 1 cup sugar, and the cream. Stir and bring mixture to a boil. Boil, stirring constantly, for 5 or 6 minutes, or until slightly thickened. Let this mixture cool.

Blend together the flour, brown sugar and the chilled butter bits in a small bowl. I use a pastry blender to make coarse crumbs. Set the springform pan on a cookie sheet to catch any drips. Now spread the raisin mixture carefully over the cheesecake. Make sure entire surface is covered. Sprinkle the flour mixture over that and broil cheesecake under a preheated broiler about 4" from the heat source for 2 or 3 minutes, or until golden and bubbly on top, but not brown. Let cheesecake cool for several minutes, then cover loosely and refrigerate for several hours, or overnight is best.

Obviously, this is very rich, so it will make many servings. This is truly as good as it sounds!

Pecan Pie

I wouldn't dare have a family Holiday meal without at least two pecan pies on the sideboard! It is one of our family's favorite pies and before the evening is over, nearly everyone has a piece. This recipe came from two sisters in my church, Mae and Kay. We have all used the recipe, or a variation of it, for years. These pies may be made and baked in advance and frozen for a week or so before you need them, but I do think that fresh-from-the-oven the day of the party is best. Have the crusts refrigerated or frozen ahead of time and add the filling and bake the day you need them. Makes two 9" pies.

6	eggs
1½	to 2 cups sugar (I use 1½ cups)
2	tablespoons flour
2	tablespoons butter, melted
1	cup light Karo syrup
1	cup dark Karo syrup
2	teaspoons vanilla extract
3	cups pecans, coarsely chopped
2	9" unbaked pastry shells

In a small bowl, combine sugar and flour, and stir until well mixed. In a fairly large bowl, beat 6 eggs. Add the sugar-flour mixture, butter, both syrups and vanilla. Stir in the pecans and divide filling between the 2 pastry shells. Bake the pies in a 325° oven for about 1 hour, or until pie middle is set.

Pecan Pie, Holiday Cheesecake and Gingerbread Boys and Girls

Holiday
Decorations
from
Oak Hill
Farm

O Christmas Trees!

Soon after Thanksgiving each year, we begin decorating three trees for Christmas. One tree is in the foyer and we call it *The Gift Tree*. *The Birds' Christmas Tree* is decorated in the dining room and *The Children's Christmas Tree* is set up in the breakfast room. Each is totally different as you'll see on the following pages, and each serves a different and specific purpose.

Long before Christmas arrives, I think about what will go on each tree and even though they have been decorated in the same theme for several years, I do occasionally add something new or different to one or all three trees as the years go by. And so, November often finds me making new ginger-bread boys, or new golden bird nests, or some other new decoration for one of the trees. I find the most important thing is to have any decorations to be added or replaced completed before the trees are set up.

I do hope that on these pages you will find one or two (or more!) ideas that you can use on your tree or trees!

The Gift Tree

The Gift Tree

This is the tree that greets family and friends as they arrive for Holiday parties or meals. It is the *true* Christmas tree in the house because all presents are placed under this tree for Christmas Eve or Christmas Day. The tree glows with tiny white lights and an assortment of antique Christmas ornaments. Color is added with bunches of dried statices (purple, pink, yellow, white) and wired gold mesh ribbon bows. Also adorning this tree are mini potpourri wreaths. A lovely renaissance-style angel is perched on top. A crazy quilt acts as the tree skirt. A child's antique ice cream table is set for tea in front of the tree and an assortment of bears, dolls and rabbits have been invited to join the festivities. An old Battenberg lace cloth covers the table and one of the mini potpourri wreaths is used as the candle ring on the brass candlestick.

Following are the recipes and methods for making both mini potpourri wreaths and mini spice wreaths.

Mini Potpourri Wreaths

For one 2¹/₂" to 3" wreath, you'll need:

1   to 1¹/₄ cups potpourri (the prettier the potpourri, the prettier the wreath!)
1   tablespoon white glue (such as Elmer's)
1   tablespoon water
1   2¹/₂" to 3" ring mold

🎄 Grease a 2¹/₂" to 3" ring mold with soft oleo or a nonstick vegetable spray. I use a doughnut cutter with the handle removed so the cutter will lay flat upside down.

🎄 Use a cottage cheese carton (or some other disposable container) and mix the water and white glue together to make a thin paste.

🎄 Add the potpourri and stir well to coat the leaves and petals with the thin glue mixture.

🎄 Pack mixture into the prepared mold and tamp it down with your fingertips — don't worry about seeing the glue because it will dry clear.

🎄 Drizzle the glue left in the container over the potpourri mixture in the mold.

🎄 Let mold set for about 6 hours. Run a table knife around the inside and outside edges of the mold and gently ease wreath from mold.

🎄 Let dry for several days, turning occasionally to dry evenly on both sides.

🎄 Because the glue mixture coats the potpourri, the wreath may lose its fragrance. After the wreath is thoroughly dry, add a drop or 2 of essential oil (your choice) to each wreath.

🎄 To store, wrap each wreath in plastic wrap and keep out of direct light until ready to use at Holiday time.

🎄 When you "undecorate" the tree, rewrap wreaths in plastic wrap and place them in a covered box away from heat and light.

Paddington Bear and friend Big Rabbit are ready for tea. A mini potpourri wreath becomes a candle ring on their tea table. And a mini spice wreath is a napkin ring.

Mini Spice Wreaths

I have found many uses for these little wreaths. Besides hanging them on a tree, I also use them as package tie-ons. I especially like to use them as napkin rings. Not only did I use them on the bears' tea table, they are on the table for Christmas Eve at Oak Hill Farm (see page 38).

For one 2¹/₂" to 3" wreath, you'll need:

³/₄	cup whole spices (see below)
1	teaspoon ground cinnamon
1	tablespoon white glue (such as Elmer's)
1	tablespoon water
1	2¹/₂" to 3" ring mold

🎄 There are no exact measurements for the whole spice mixture. Combine **whole cloves, broken cinnamon sticks** (put in a plastic bag and hit with a hammer or wooden rolling pin), **whole allspice, whole nutmeg** (also broken into pieces) and **dried orange or lemon peel pieces. Chopped whole vanilla beans** and other **aromatic spices** may be added.

🎄 Grease the ring mold with soft oleo or a nonstick vegetable spray.

🎄 Use a cottage cheese carton and mix the water and glue together to make a thin paste.

🎄 Add the spice mixture and the ground cinnamon. Stir to coat all the mixture.

🎄 Pack mixture into the prepared mold and tamp it down.

🎄 Drizzle any glue left in the container over the spices. The glue will dry clear.

🎄 Let wreath set for 6 hours.

🎄 Remove wreath from mold and let it dry thoroughly — a week at least — turning it occasionally.

The Birds'
Christmas Tree

The Birds' Christmas Tree

I simply love the tree in our dining room! It is not as large as the other trees. It nestles into the corner between the old pine cupboard and the carpenter's bench which acts as our serving table or buffet. There are wonderful things on this tree — even fresh flowers!

We light the tree with tiny white lights, add a few white grosgrain wired ribbon bows and hang dehydrator-dried orange slices from the branches. They look like tiny stained glass windows! Besides a dozen fresh blooms (fragrant white and yellow freesias) in water balls (these are actually little vases that tie onto the branches), we also decorate the tree with beautiful dried hydrangea blooms.

This has become our bird tree! We load the branches with colorful birds — all shapes, sizes and colors, put a few of the little birds in golden bird nests and give them some gingerbread birdhouses to call home! The tree topper is made of birch tree branches gathered from the yard, sprayed a bright gold and randomly tucked into the tree top. The tree looks woodsy and at the same time somewhat elegant! I love to add a few of these gold branches to the greenery that tops the antique cupboards. The tree skirt is an old quilt top that never got quilted. It does double duty as a table cloth other times of the year.

This tree is truly for the birds! On the following pages, learn how to make golden bird nests and gingerbread birdhouses. Note also in the picture how beautiful the dried orange slices, dried hydrangea blooms and fresh flowers are on the tree.

Golden Bird Nests

The children or grandchildren will have fun helping make these little nests. Supplies needed are: **muffin pan, nonstick vegetable cooking spray, dried grasses, white glue, plastic cups, gold spray paint** *and* **spring clip clothespins**.

- Gather grass clippings (yes, the ones from the lawn mower) and let them dry. I spread them on an old sheet. They'll dry in 1 or 2 days.

- Lightly spray each muffin cup with the nonstick spray. Turn muffin pans upside down after they're sprayed so excess can drip out.

- Press the grass (use plenty) into the muffin cups. Drizzle white glue over the bottom and sides of the grass — it dries clear.

- Choose a plastic cup with a bottom that will fit inside the muffin cup. Spray the bottom and up the sides a little with the cooking spray. Set this cup **inside** the muffin cup and press and twist gently — this forms the nest shape. Carefully remove the plastic cup and let nests dry for a couple of hours.

- Carefully remove each nest and now put them upside down on the greased bottoms of the plastic cups, 1 for each nest. These are fragile at this point.

- Drizzle more glue over the upside down nests and let them dry for another 2 or 3 hours.

- Put a strip of glue on the bottom of each nest and set a spring clip clothespin on the glue. Gently press down on the clothespin so that it makes good contact with the glue. Let dry in this position for 6 to 8 hours.

- When nests are dry and still upside down, spray each nest and the clothespin with gold paint. This "glues" the nest together.

- When paint is thoroughly dry, set nests off the plastic cups, turn upright and spray the inside of each nest.

- Set a bird (check florist or craft store for these colorful little birds) inside each nest and clip the nest to a Christmas tree branch.

- To store, lay nests, clothespin side down, in a deep suit or shirt box, put lid on and label "fragile." I guess they aren't too fragile though — some of my nests are at least 15 years old, so they will last a long time if stored properly.

- These little nests are ragged and uneven looking, but they do look like the real thing, except for the gold paint!

Gingerbread Birdhouses

These came about quite by accident. I had some gingerbread house dough left over and because I wanted birdhouses on the dining room tree, I decided to cut out a pattern and glue one together to see if it would work. I made a house from the pattern and it worked beautifully! These wonderful and fragrant little houses are decorated with ornamental icing. I use the gingerbread house dough recipe with permission from Foods of the World Recipes, The Cooking of Germany © 1969 Time-Life Books, Inc. *Refer to this recipe on page 84 in the Gingerbread House section of this book. One recipe of the dough will make four birdhouses.*

The following illustration shows how to cut out the pattern. Lightweight cardboard works best for the pattern.

Pattern For A Gingerbread Birdhouse

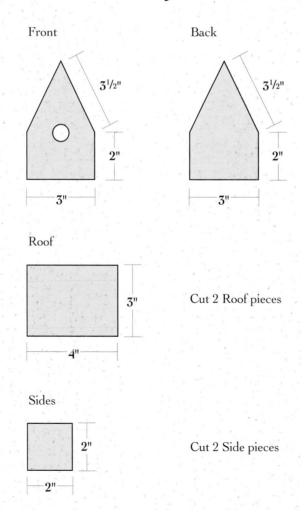

Front

$3\frac{1}{2}$"

2"

3"

Back

$3\frac{1}{2}$"

2"

3"

Roof

3"

4"

Cut 2 Roof pieces

Sides

2"

2"

Cut 2 Side pieces

🎄 Make gingerbread house dough. Follow instructions on pages 84-87.

🎄 While gingerbread is still warm and still in the pan, lay pattern pieces on the gingerbread and cut around each piece with a sharp knife.

🎄 Let pieces cool thoroughly, then remove from pan.

🎄 With a hot glue gun, glue the front, back and 2 sides together to make a house shape. When glue is set, glue the roof pieces in place. Gently hold roof pieces in place until glue sets — a minute or so. Set house aside and let glue dry thoroughly before decorating the house. By the way, there is no bottom in this house — you'll see why later.

🎄 To decorate 6 or 8 birdhouses such as the ones in the photo, make ½ batch of ornamental icing. The recipe is on page 87. Use the photo as a guide and spread the icing on the house using a regular table knife. Let icing dry several hours or until it is rock-hard.

🎄 Use a small drill bit (in the electric drill) and drill a hole in each roof half — the holes opposite each other, near the top and centered between front and back so the house will hang balanced.

🎄 For a hanger, use a piece of raffia, heavy twine, or Christmas ribbon and poke the twine from the top of the roof down. Take other end of twine and poke it down from the top of other half of roof. Gently lay the house down on its back and pull both ends of the twine down. Tie ends in a sturdy knot — this is why house has no bottom in it! Set house back on its base and carefully pull the twine up through the roof holes. Now you have a hanger to attach the house to a tree limb.

🎄 Drill a small hole in the front of each house (under the opening), and push a 1½" long piece of cinnamon stick into the little hole. This cinnamon stick is the bird's perch.

🎄 It's a good idea to spray each finished house with shellac or polyurethane to help preserve them.

🎄 These little houses are wonderful on a tree, attached to a wreath, or used in table arrangements. They are for indoor use only and they are **not** edible.

The Children's
Christmas Tree

The Children's Christmas Tree

The children love this tree! It is bright, colorful and fragrant. We like tiny multicolored lights on this tree. It has been decorated in a red, white and gingerbread theme for several years now — we seem to like this color scheme best. Besides gingerbread boys and girls on the tree, there are two kinds of garlands. Strings of red wooden beads are one type of garland and dried apple slices are another type.

The bows on this tree are made of wired ribbon — dark green background with beautiful red apples printed on the ribbon. These look especially wonderful with the apple garlands. I recently started making applesauce and spice dough baskets for this tree and love the way they look and smell!

I found crisp white Battenberg lace stars and hearts one year and they add a splash of white to all the red and green on the tree. I have an old Battenberg lace tablecloth that has a hole on one side, but when I fold the cloth in half and shape it around the base of the tree, the hole disappears and a beautiful tree skirt emerges! Moral of the story — don't dispose of beautiful old things, even if they are damaged. There is usually some way to use them.

Since this is the tree the children love so much, we pile old toys, sleds, a rocking horse and Santas around the tree. There are even a couple of children's old rocking chairs near the tree, and more than once I've seen a grand-child in one of those chairs rocking away and dreaming of what Santa will bring.

This tree is in a corner of the breakfast room near the table. We all love to have supper here — the smell of apples and gingerbread mingle with the smell of fresh pine — **this** is Christmas!

On this tree you can see how the apple garland is sewed together. Note also the gingerbread boys and the ginger girls and the way they are "dressed." The applesauce and spice dough baskets add such a nice touch to this tree. As I'll tell you later, the baskets are filled with green moss (you could use Spanish moss if desired) and little sprigs of tallow berries which were sent to me by a friend from Louisiana.

Following are recipes and methods for making apple garlands, gingerbread boys, ginger girls and applesauce and spice dough baskets. I hope you'll make some of these things for your tree — they've got it all! They are made from natural ingredients, they are beautiful and they are fragrant.

Apple Garlands

🎄 Slice **unpeeled Red Delicious apples** from top to bottom into ¼" thick slices (set apple on a cutting board and use a rather large sharp knife). By slicing the apple from top to bottom, the apple slices will be heart-shaped.

🎄 Combine **2 cups bottled lemon juice** (such as Real Lemon) and **1 tablespoon salt** in a medium-sized bowl.

🎄 Soak several apple slices at a time in the lemon mixture for 3 to 4 minutes.

🎄 Remove the slices, shake off excess moisture and place them on a cake rack or a large cookie sheet in a 175° oven. Dry with oven door ajar for 6 to 12 hours, or until slices begin to curl slightly and feel dry and leathery. Do **not** brown. Turn slices often.

🎄 Variation: Dry lemon and salt-treated slices in a food dehydrator which will take 4 to 6 hours. Follow your dehydrator drying instructions for drying fruit slices. Of the 2 methods, I find the dehydrator-dried slices are superior.

🎄 For a garland like the ones seen on *The Children's Tree*, "sew" the slices together. Use dark green garden jute twine or dark green acrylic yarn — the green looks good with the red-rimmed apples. Thread this twine into a large eye needle and "sew" the dried apple slices together.
Bring twine up through the back of apple slice, across the middle and back down through the slice, similar to the illustration. Tie a knot on either side of the slice to help stabilize it.

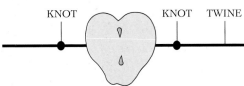

🎄 Go back and look at the full page picture of the children's tree. Cynthia Bookwalter, who designed the ginger girls on page 68, also made the angel-doll tree topper. It is so unique because she holds in her left hand the apple garland that winds around the tree!

🎄 Be sure to dry some extra apple slices to add to Holiday potpourris or to glue on a wreath. They are beautiful.

🎄 "Sew" some of these apple slices (as well as dehydrator dried orange slices) together and fit a circle of them around fat candles or glass votive candle holders.

🎄 Glue a dried apple or orange slice to a place card for the Holiday table. There are so many ways to use them.

Applesauce and Spice Dough Baskets

These baskets are made from an applesauce and spice dough recipe. They dry naturally — they are **not** baked. I've had some ornaments made from this recipe for years, but only recently experimented with the baskets. The baskets are very fragrant and durable if handled carefully. They look great on the tree with the gingerbread people.

It does take time and effort to make these baskets, but if stored properly, they should last several years. In other words, you shouldn't have to make these every year.

I wanted to put something special and also something light in color in the baskets so when a friend from Louisiana, Joy Mabry, sent some tallow berries, I knew the "something special" had been found! Tallow berries are white, very hard and very durable.

Here is the recipe I use for these great little baskets:

4	ounces ground cinnamon
1	tablespoon ground cloves
1	tablespoon ground nutmeg
$^3/_4$	cup (plus a little more) applesauce
2	tablespoons white glue (such as Elmer's)
	foil baking cups

Combine spices in a medium bowl.

Add applesauce and glue; stir to make a pliable dough. ($^3/_4$ cup applesauce isn't quite enough, I find, but 1 cup is too much, so start with $^3/_4$ cup and add 1 tablespoon at a time until dough loses its stickiness — however, it must not be dry either or the strips will crack.)

Divide each ball of dough into 4 or 5 pieces. Roll each piece on a lightly floured board (the rolling pin must be floured also). Roll to no less than 1/4" thickness. Try to roll into a 6" to 8" square.

With a ruler, mark dough into 1/2" wide x 6" long strips. Gather scraps and put back into the bowl. They can be worked into the remaining dough. Note: I wanted about 20 baskets for the tree, so I made 3 recipes of the dough.

It will take 6 strips of the dough to form each basket. Carefully lay 4 strips, one at a time, over the bottom of each upside down foil cup. (At the grocery store, I found foil individual cupcake cups, 8 to a package. They are 3" in diameter and 1 1/2" tall, the exact size I wanted the baskets to be.) Lay the first strip on and put a dot of white glue in the center where the second strip will crisscross it. Do the same with 2 more strips.

This is how to lay strips of dough over the upside down cup.

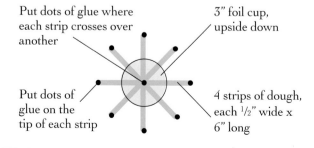

Put dots of glue where each strip crosses over another

3" foil cup, upside down

Put dots of glue on the tip of each strip

4 strips of dough, each 1/2" wide x 6" long

🎄 Gently mold strips down the side of the cup to make basket shape.

🎄 Put a dot of white glue on the tip of each strip (it will dry clear).

🎄 Lay 2 more 6" strips around the bottom of the cup. Join these 2 strips together with dots of glue. Now press the 2 strips gently, but firmly, to each hanging strip. This forms the rim on top of the basket.

This is how a completed basket looks as it is drying on an upside down foil baking cup.

🎄 Do not disturb the baskets for at least 4 or 5 days. They must be dry and hard before attempting to ease them out of the cups.

🎄 I decorated each basket with a little green moss in the bottom and filled the basket with short pieces of tallow berries. Don't forget that these baskets must be handled carefully! If you don't have tallow berries, use pepperberries, rose hips, or pretty artificial berries in the baskets.

🎄 Tie ribbon or piece of raffia on each side of the basket to form a loop and hang on the tree.

🎄 After Christmas, carefully wrap each basket in plastic wrap and store in a covered box away from heat and light. If properly stored and handled, they should last a long time.

By the way, don't worry if all the strips aren't perfectly spaced, or if the basket rims are a little crooked. These are homemade, after all, and shouldn't be absolutely perfect! The little imperfections in all these homemade decorations — whether they be the baskets, the gingerbread boys, or whatever — only add to their charm and prove they are not store-bought clones of each other!

Variation: Make tree ornaments with this same dough recipe. After the dough is rolled out, dip the desired cookie cutter into flour and cut into shapes. Make a hole in the top of each ornament with a toothpick. Transfer the cut-out ornaments to cookie sheets and let them dry at room temperature for at least a week. (Let dry for 2 days undisturbed, then turn ornaments over each day to dry evenly.) Thread ribbon through the hole in the ornament and hang on the tree, use as a package trim, or give some to a lucky friend. One recipe of Applesauce and Spice Dough will make 1$\frac{1}{2}$ to 2 dozen small- to average-sized ornaments.

Old Fashioned Gingerbread Boys

I can't imagine Christmas without gingerbread boys on the tree! When the Holidays are over, I wrap each cookie in plastic wrap, lay them in a box, cover the box and store in a cool, dark place — the freezer if I have room. When I take them out the next year, they are perfect.

Besides making some for yourself, a box of decorated cookies would make a great gift for your child's busy teacher — actually, anybody on your list would love them! Read through the entire recipe before starting.

1	cup butter, at room temperature
1	cup light brown sugar, firmly packed
1	cup dark molasses
	grated peel of 1 lemon
	grated peel of 1 orange
1	tablespoon ground cinnamon
1	tablespoon ground ginger
1½	teaspoons baking soda
½	teaspoon salt
2	eggs, beaten
4	to 6 cups sifted flour

🎄 Cream butter and sugar in a large bowl until light and fluffy.

🎄 Bring molasses to a boil in a small saucepan.

🎄 Add molasses to the creamed mixture and mix thoroughly. Add peels, spices, baking soda and salt. Beat in eggs.

🎄 Measure and add sifted flour, 1 cup at a time, until dough is smooth, soft and pliable. (If measured and added properly, all 6 cups will be used.)

🎄 Wrap dough in plastic wrap and chill for an hour.

🎄 Preheat oven to 350°.

🎄 Work with part of the dough at a time. Keep rest of dough refrigerated. Roll dough ⅛" thick on a lightly floured board. Use desired cutter and carefully lift the cookie to an ungreased baking sheet.

🎄 Punch a hole in head of gingerbread boy with a toothpick or small nail so a ribbon or string can go through it.

🎄 Bake at 350° for 15 minutes, or until firm to touch.

🎄 The number of ornaments from each recipe depends on size and shape of cutters used.

🎄 If you wish to decorate the cookies with raisins or hard candies, add the eyes, mouth, and buttons, and gently press them into the dough before baking.

🎄 If you wish to frost the cookies, combine **2 egg whites, pinch of salt, 3 cups sifted confectioners' sugar,** and **1 teaspoon lemon juice** in an electric mixer bowl. Beat the mixture until it stands in stiff peaks. If necessary, add a little more sugar to make frosting stiffer. Pack this mixture into a pastry tube and add eyes, mouth, and buttons to the baked, cooled cookies.

🎄 Last but not least, you may wish to decorate the baked, cooled cookies with acrylic paints as you see them on our tree. We chose white for the eyes, mouth, fingers, toes and buttons and added a little red heart to each. You can do this yourself or, if you're lucky like me, you'll have an artist friend like Mae DeBord paint them for you!

🎄 To preserve the cookies, spray with shellac or polyurethane. Spray one side, dry thoroughly, turn cookies and spray other side. If possible, hang the cookies after spraying so they'll dry evenly and thoroughly.

Well-Dressed Ginger Girls

My friend, Cynthia Bookwalter, was bemoaning the fact one day that she had overbaked a batch of gingerbread boys and girls. Not wanting to throw them away, she thought there was surely something interesting she could do with them. Well, there was and these delightful very well-dressed ginger girls were born! They look absolutely wonderful on the tree with gingerbread boys. Following is Cynthia's method for making them.

🎄 Make your favorite **gingerbread cookie recipe** (the preceding one for gingerbread boys works fine) and cut and bake gingerbread girls. Be sure to bake them the full baking time and even a little longer so that they are very well done and quite hard. Also be sure to make a hole in the top of each head before baking if you plan to hang them.

🎄 For decorating the girls, you will need **scraps of prepasted wallpaper, a glass of warm water, a pair of small sharp scissors** and **scraps of old laces and ribbons, buttons,** and even **tiny dried flowers and berries.**

🎄 Trace the ginger girl, face down, on the back of a wallpaper scrap. Do not trace around the head of the girl unless you want her face wallpapered. Simply stop at the shoulder on each side and after removing the cookie from the wallpaper, draw in the line that forms the neckline of the dress. Cut out the dress and drop it into the glass of warm water. Count to 10 or 15 and remove the dress from the water. Immediately place the dress on the front of a baked and cooled cookie. Using your fingers and a paper towel, pat the dress in place. Smooth the paper being careful not to press too hard (they are cookies, after all, and could break). If the cookie does break, simply glue back together with your hot glue gun.

🎄 After the wallpaper has dried, use your imagination to accessorize your ginger girls. Add a lace ruffle at the neckline, glue tiny buttons down the front, glue on a "belt" of ribbon, attach beads for a necklace. Paint facial features on if you like. The longer you work on these, the better they'll get and each girl is sure to be unique.

🎄 If you intend to keep the girls for more than one season, spray them with a satin finish polyurethane after the wallpaper dresses are dry and before you add the lace, buttons and decorations.

🎄 Be creative with your cookie cutter collection. Try wallpapering and decorating stars, moons, angels, birds, trees and other shapes. They can make very original Christmas ornaments that you, your family and your friends will all enjoy.

Christmas Wreaths

Wreaths come in all shapes and sizes for our Holiday decorating. We have a fresh or dried advent wreath for the season as well as a fabulous fresh rosemary wreath, and even a toy wreath. There is also a special wreath for the kitchen window and another for the fireplace wall. We use everything from real greenery wreath forms to grapevines, twigs, wet oasis, styrofoam and artificial greenery. Some of our wreaths hang, and some are used as candle rings or punch bowl rings.

I'll tell you how we make our wreaths on the following pages. None of them are difficult and it is so satisfying to create your own — whether it be a wreath made totally from scratch, or whether you take a store-bought one and add your own touches.

The Advent Wreath

The advent wreath, whether it be a fresh or dried one, is a beautiful and meaningful decoration for your home or church at Holiday time. This tradition probably originated in Germany hundreds of years ago.

The first candle of the season is to be lit on Advent Sunday, an event that marks the first of four weeks (Sundays) before Jesus' birth. The most significant meaning of advent is that of joyful anticipation. Hence, at some time during the advent season, you will no doubt sing or hear the old hymn, *"O Come, O Come Emmanuel."*

The greenery, herbs, candles, dried flowers and ribbons are the same for a fresh wreath or a dried wreath. First, I'll give you the meanings and significance of the various items used to make a fresh or dried wreath, then I'll tell you how to make each kind.

There are many symbols and meanings for the advent wreath. They include:

1. THE CIRCLE — The circle here is the **wreath**. It is a universal symbol of **eternity.**
2. THE EVERGREENS — **Juniper or cedar** are usually used. They suggest **life and hope.**
3. THE BURNING CANDLES* — They represent **Christ** as the **light of the world.**
    PROPHET'S CANDLE — A **purple or white** candle representing the **period of waiting.**
    BETHLEHEM CANDLE — A **purple or white** candle representing the **preparation to receive the Child.**
    SHEPHERD'S CANDLE —A **purple or white** candle representing the **sharing of Christ.**
    ANGEL CANDLE — A **pink or white** candle to represent **rejoicing**.
    CHRIST'S CANDLE — If used, this candle is **white or purple** and represents the **Child's birth.**
4. EVERLASTING FLOWERS — These represent **everlasting life.**
5. PURPLE (color) — Whether it be candles, ribbons or flowers, purple represents the **holy** aspect of Advent.
6. PINK (color) — Whether it be candles, ribbons or flowers, this color represents **joy.**

*Following is a list of the numbers and colors of candles I have seen used in these wreaths:

FOUR CANDLES — Three candles are purple and one pink. (This is the way I do my wreath.)

FIVE CANDLES — Three candles are purple, one pink and one large white candle for the middle. The large white candle represents Jesus.

FIVE CANDLES — Four candles are white and one large purple candle for the middle. The purple candle represents Jesus.

If a large candle is used in the middle of the wreath, it is lit on Christmas Eve or Christmas Day.

The everlasting flowers and ribbons used in these wreaths:

For either a fresh or dried wreath, everlasting flowers such as the statices, straw flowers, or globe amaranth blooms are added for color and filler. The narrow satin ribbons are tied to each candle base. Leave tails on the ribbons to hang down from the wreath. Other good filler materials are artemisias, such as silver king, silver queen or silver brocade, or sweet Annie sprigs. I try to use purple statice pieces and pink and purple globe amaranth blooms to help carry out the pink and purple theme.

Traditional herbs and their meanings in the advent wreath are:

ROSEMARY (*Rosmarinus officinalis*) — the herb of **remembrance**
THYME (*Thymus vulgaris*) — the symbol of **bravery of the child**
SAGE (*Salvia officinalis*) — the herb of **immortality**
LAVENDER (*Lavandula, many species*) — the herb of **purity and virtue**
RUE (*Ruta graveolens*) — the herb of **grace**
COSTMARY (*Chrysanthemum balsamita*) — the herb of **everlasting life**
HOREHOUND (*Marrubium vulgare*) — this herb represents **good health**

If I have a choice between a fresh herbal wreath and a dried herbal wreath, I would choose the fresh one. It is truly a thing of beauty and fragrance.

The fresh wreath pictured was designed by my friend, Don Haynie, of Buffalo Springs Herb Farm, Raphine, Virginia. The herbs are placed in wet oasis and the wreath will stay beautiful throughout the Holiday season. Keep the oasis moist at all times. This means the wreath must be placed on a large, waterproof tray to protect the table top. Oasis, by the way, is available from garden supply stores or from your florist.

The Advent Wreath with Fresh Herbs

To make an advent wreath with fresh herbs, you will need the following supplies: a 14" to 16" box wire frame, floral foam (oasis), a shallow waterproof tray, fresh evergreen pieces, the appropriate fresh herbs, candle holders that will push into the foam, candles and about 4 yards each of narrow pink and purple satin ribbons.

Following is the basic method of creating a fresh herbal wreath, such as the one pictured.

- For the base, use a 14" or 16" box wire frame available from your florist or florist supply.

- Cut floral foam (oasis) to fit the frame.

- Lay wreath form into a shallow waterproof tray and wet the foam thoroughly.

- Insert 6" to 8" pieces of juniper, cedar, or some of both, around the outside rim of the wreath. Place smaller pieces (3" to 4" long) around the inside rim.

- Place 4 candle sockets in the oasis an equal distance apart.

- Place little bundles of fresh broad-leaf herbs (sage, for example) on top and press the stems into the wet foam. Fill the spaces with smaller leaf herbs (thyme or rosemary, for example). Try to alternate herbs considering leaf texture and color.

- Place everlastings (such as globe amaranth or statice) in groups at the base of each candle socket.

- Insert candles and tie narrow pink and purple satin ribbons around the base of each candle. Leave tails of 12" or more on each ribbon.

The wreath looks best if displayed on a small table. The wreath should actually cover the table top so the ribbon streamers can hang down.

The Advent Wreath with Dried Herbs

I realize that in cold regions of the country, we may not have fresh herbs to gather for a fresh advent wreath, so the herbs must be gathered in late summer, sorted into bunches, hung and dried. Any time after the herbs are dried, the wreath can be made and stored for advent use. Store the wreath flat, not hanging.

To make a dried herbal advent wreath, choose a 14" or 16" styrofoam wreath form, craft pins or fine gauge floral wire (available from the florist or the craft shop), evergreens, the appropriate herbs, candle holders that will push down into the styrofoam (again, check the florist or craft shop), candles and about 4 yards each of narrow pink and purple satin ribbons.

Following is the basic method for making an advent wreath with dried herbs.

- Lay small juniper or cedar branches on the outside and inside perimeters of the wreath. I use fresh pieces of greenery. They dry naturally on the wreath. Attach these pieces, one at a time, with a craft pin or the wire. Continue in one direction around the wreath, covering the stem and craft pin with a new evergreen piece as you go.

- Attach little bundles of dried herbs with pins or wire and completely cover the wreath.

- Space the candle holders equally around the wreath.

- Place everlastings (such as globe amaranth or statice) in groups at the base of each candle socket.

- Insert candles and tie narrow pink and purple satin ribbons around the base of each candle. Leave tails of 12" or more on each ribbon.

Think about an advent wreath as you plant your herb garden in the spring. Do plant the traditional herbs of the wreath and enjoy a part of your herb garden throughout the Holiday season.

The Holly and the Ivy Wreath

Two other plants I associate with Christmas are holly and ivy. The advantage here is that both are probably more readily available than rosemary, so if you can't make the rosemary wreath, the holly and ivy are next best.

- Decide on the size wreath you would like to make. Fit a box wire frame into a waterproof tray or saucer.

- Fill the frame with florist foam and wet the foam thoroughly.

- Push sprigs of fresh holly into the foam — you may need to wear gloves because it's sharp and spiny.

- Fill in spaces with nice trailing sprigs of ivy, also pushed into the foam. Be sure to use plenty of plant material to make a good, full wreath.

- Don't let foam dry out — keep watered.

- A red bow looks best on this wreath to accent the red holly berries. This is a beautiful, fresh wreath.

The rosemary wreath on the coffee table in front of the fireplace is one of our most beautiful decorations. When we brush against it, the wonderful pine-like fragrance is released and fills the room. To me, rosemary is truly the Christmas herb.

Fresh Rosemary Wreath

This wreath was designed to fit the base of an antique crackle glass globe. The globe was one of those once-in-a-lifetime finds at a yard sale. The old gas light fixture was long gone and the seller had no use for the globe. From that day, the globe with a big candle (red for Christmas) has been at home on our coffee table. The globe is surrounded with other wreaths during the year, but at Christmas time, it is absolutely at its best surrounded with rosemary!

The wreath is made very much like the fresh advent wreath. Since my globe is large, we need to use an 18" frame with a 14" opening.

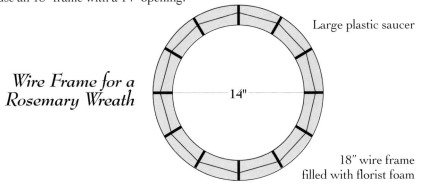

Wire Frame for a Rosemary Wreath

Large plastic saucer

14"

18" wire frame filled with florist foam

❦ I use an 18" diameter plastic saucer (from a large plastic planting pot) and lay the box wire frame inside it.

❦ Cut florist foam to fit the frame. Wet foam thoroughly.

❦ I use 6" to 8" sprigs of fresh rosemary and fill the frame full. Leave a space on one side for a big bow.

❦ Attach bow and fill in any spaces with more rosemary.

❦ I turn a deep, small saucer upside down in the middle of the plastic tray and set the globe and candle on it. This elevates them above the water.

❦ Keep the wreath well watered. Water must come up to the bottom of the florist foam to keep the sprigs from drying out This glorious wreath will stay that way (glorious, that is) for a month or more.

About now, you're probably wondering where I got all the rosemary since it is the dead of the winter in Indiana! I have nurtured a most wonderful rosemary plant for 4 years now. It grows and thrives on our sunny deck from April through October. It is planted in soilless mix in a very large pot. While it's on the deck, it gets watered and fed regularly. Before the first hard frost, I take this plant to a friend's greenhouse. And so, early in December we trim 6" to 8" pieces to bring home to make the wreath with. I keep any sprigs not used for the wreath in a plastic bag with the stems wrapped in wet paper towels. I use these sprigs for other decorations throughout the house.

If you have only a small amount of rosemary at your disposal, make a small wreath and use it as a candle ring. But I'd suggest you work at growing a nice large plant — the rewards are tremendous.

The Toy Wreath

I bought this wreath many years ago from a retail store. It is a large grapevine wreath that has an artificial greenery garland wrapped around it. When I bought it, there was a wooden Santa attached to it, a couple of bears, and two or three other toys.

Each year I have added something to the wreath. It was often a toy that no one played with anymore, but it was too good to dispose of, or it had sentimental value. One day one of the grandchildren said she loved my "toy wreath," so it has been called that ever since.

Some of the things I've added over the years are an old, well-worn and, obviously, well-loved bear, another bear sitting in his little red chair reading all about Christmas, a gingerbread boy I embroidered on a bright red piece of fabric and framed in green, and, the best of all, an old, very long-legged rabbit in a red and white polka dot dress. My husband, Dick, gave her to me for Christmas one year in a brown paper grocery sack — no wrapping paper and no ribbons. He said she was really too homely to wrap! But she is one of my favorite things and she is displayed for all to see on this wreath. Color is added to the wreath with dark red wooden berries and a big, dark red bow.

The wreath has hung in our dining room above the serving table for many Christmases. I think we would greatly miss it if it weren't there.

Decorators tell us to gather things into a collection and display them together. What better way to display old toys or dolls that the children have outgrown than on such a wreath? You'll be surprised at the memories this wreath will bring back each year. Those memories can only get better with the passage of time.

Birdhouses around the Toy Wreath

Because the dining room has become our "bird" room at Christmas time, we decided to surround the toy wreath with birdhouses. We think they make a nice frame for the wreath. We added fresh greenery around the house bases, wove a string of tiny, white lights into the greenery, and perched two or three small, red cardinals on the greenery — they are Indiana's state bird! This is all placed at the back of the serving table. We add candlelight to complete the festive setting.

Our birdhouses are decorative only. I found them at a local florist for only a few dollars each.

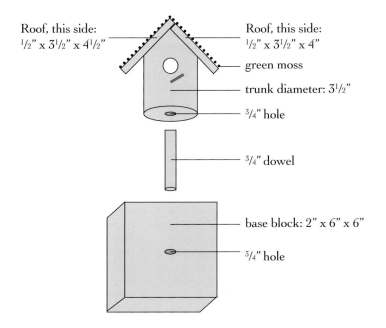

Roof, this side:
½" x 3½" x 4½"

Roof, this side:
½" x 3½" x 4"

green moss

trunk diameter: 3½"

¾" hole

¾" dowel

base block: 2" x 6" x 6"

¾" hole

For do-it-yourselfers, each house is a piece of round tree trunk (the conifer family has nice bark, so trees in that group are a good choice).

We placed 5 houses around the wreath (see toy wreath picture). The dowel heights for our houses are 4", 7", 10", 17" and 22". The dowel rods are ¾" in diameter. See illustration for house, roof and base sizes. We glued green moss on each birdhouse roof, but Spanish moss would work also.

Take the same ¾" drill bit used to make the dowel rod holes and bore an opening into each house — it only needs to be an inch or so deep. You may want to paint the inside of the opening with black or brown paint so the raw wood doesn't show. If desired, add a bird perch below each opening. The perches on our houses are horseshoe nails, but you may choose to use regular nails.

We stained our dowel rods and bases brown to blend with the color of the houses. They could also be painted.

Make these houses as plain or as decorated as you like, or make them to match your decorating theme. I think you'll like these houses so much you won't want to use them just at Christmas! They would make wonderful accents in a sun room, on a screened porch, in a family room, or wherever, any time of the year.

This wreath was designed by a friend, Carl Taylor. It is literally made with
odds and ends. When the decorating is finished (is it really ever finished?!)
and I have a few dried orange and apple slices left, two or three pomegranates,
some pepperberries and bits and pieces of many of the other things I use for
decorations, then I gather all these things together and make this colorful
wreath for the kitchen window. If you don't use a twig wreath, an artificial
wreath is a good choice. Add a bow, if desired, but I like this wreath without
one. Any way you decorate it, this is a beautiful and fragrant wreath.

A Wreath for the Kitchen

Following is a list of supplies and ingredients I use. If you don't have all these things, substitute your own decorations.

Supplies/Equipment

hot glue gun
twig wreath, about 16" to 18" in diameter, or whatever size fits your window
sprigs of preserved cedar
bay leaves
cinnamon sticks
whole star anise
small to medium pine cones
sweet gum balls
dried pomegranates
dried hydrangea bloom pieces
pepperberries
dried orange slices (dehydrator dried are best)
dried apple slices (dehydrator dried are best)
1 golden bird nest (see page 57)
1 or 2 colorful artificial birds
gingerbread hearts or other Christmas cookies
1 gingerbread birdhouse (see pages 58-59)

Lay the wreath form on a large piece of foil or waxed paper to catch any glue drips.

Glue cedar pieces and bay leaves on first.

Add a few cinnamon sticks and whole star anise, then finish with cones, dried fruits, dried or wooden berries, dried flowers, and shellacked or varnished gingerbread hearts or other Christmas-shaped cookies.

Tuck a little golden bird nest into the wreath and add a bird or two to a twig branch.

Attach a gingerbread birdhouse, or any small birdhouse, for the final touch.

To make your kitchen (or wherever you hang your wreath) smell absolutely wonderful, add a drop or two of cinnamon oil to one of the cinnamon sticks.

This wreath looks beautiful over your mantel or on your front door.

The Mantel Wreath

The wreath on the fireplace wall changes occasionally. It isn't the same each year. This was the year for pepperberries. The pepper tree is from South America. It was introduced into California as an ornamental. The tree has graceful pendulous branches and beautiful rose-colored berries. I ordered the pepperberries from Mirsky's of Beaverton, Oregon, and was delighted with the beauty and quality. The mantel is draped with a heavy fresh Douglas fir garland. Woven into that is a pine cone garland. I accented the greenery with little bunches of pepperberries and gold painted birch tree branches. And what could be prettier than polished brass candlesticks and garnet red candles at Christmastime?

Here is how to make the wreath. It's very simple, but very beautiful.

- We use a 24" fresh evergreen wreath for the base. The wreath is mostly fresh balsam with a little white pine added for texture.

- Lay wreath flat and with a hot glue gun, attach short stemmed bunches of pepperberries in a circle around the middle of the wreath. Use plenty of berries for a big jolt of color.

- Attach your prettiest bow, preferably one with some gold on it. The candlelight makes the gold branches and the gold in the bow sparkle.

Variation: Glue the berries on an artificial wreath for use more than one season.
After Christmas, lay the artificial wreath in a large flat box. Cover it with tissue paper and store in a room away from sunlight.

The Gingerbread House*

I'll never forget the first gingerbread house I made many years ago! It was lopsided and the decorations on it were just awful! But it got better each time I made one and now we consider it a highlight of our Christmas decorating. I clipped the recipe from a magazine more than 20 years ago and have basically followed that recipe all these years. Over the years, I've watched the gingerbread houses (in magazine articles)

become great works of art which surely demand untold hours of the house builder's time. Even though I admire these intricate gingerbread structures, in truth, I love this simple little peak-roofed cottage the best. Children who come to visit during the Holidays call it Hansel and Gretel's house.

We set our decorated house on a large board, add shrubbery, trees and even little people and a snowman to the outside. When we're finished, we have a landscaped cottage dripping with "snow" and bright candies and peppermint shrubs. It is a great winter wonderland scene "brought inside" for all to enjoy.

The following recipe and method are adapted from one of the *Foods of the World* series published by Time-Life Books, Inc.

*from *Foods of the World Recipes: The Cooking of Germany* © 1969 Time-Life Books, Inc. Used with permission.

Gingerbread House Dough

Read through the entire recipe before starting.

6	cups sifted flour
6	tablespoons baking powder
1½	teaspoons ground cinnamon
1	teaspoon ground ginger
1	teaspoon ground cloves
¼	teaspoon ground nutmeg
⅛	teaspoon salt
¾	cup honey
1¾	cups sugar
¼	cup butter or margarine
1	tablespoon grated lemon peel
⅓	cup lemon juice
1	egg
1	egg yolk
	Patterns cut from cardboard (see diagram)
	Ornamental frosting (recipe follows)
	Hard candies for decorations
	Peppermint trees and shrubs (recipe follows)

Prepare the dough recipe 3 times for a complete gingerbread house. Prepare 1 pan at a time and cut and cool pieces. Follow this procedure 2 more times. Cut out cardboard patterns following this diagram:

Back	Front	Side walls (cut 2)	Roof halves (cut 2)	Chimney (cut 2)	Posts (cut 4)

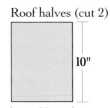

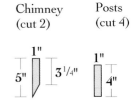

Method for preparing the dough:

🍪 Grease and flour a 17" x 11" x 1" baking pan. Set pan aside.

🍪 Sift the dry ingredients together in a large bowl. Set aside.

🍪 In a heavy Dutch oven, bring honey, sugar and butter to a boil over high heat — about 400°. Boil about 3 to 5 minutes, stirring constantly, until sugar is dissolved and butter is melted.

🍪 Remove mixture from heat and cool for 10 minutes, stirring occasionally.

🍪 Stir in lemon peel and juice. Cool 5 minutes longer.

🍪 Stir in egg and egg yolk.

🍪 Heat oven to 325°.

🍪 With a heavy wooden spoon, stir 2 cups of the flour mixture into the honey mixture. Stir vigorously to blend smooth. Add remaining flour mixture and mix well. Mixture will be dry and crumbly and hard to stir at this point.

🍪 Turn dough onto a floured board. Flour your hands and press dough into a ball. Knead 10 or 12 times to make a smooth ball.

🍪 Place dough in prepared pan and press it evenly into the pan working from the center and pressing to the corners. Keep flouring your hands as you work the dough into the pan. (Spreading the dough evenly into the pan is one of the hardest jobs in making the house.) Don't worry if dough is uneven and lumpy in the pan, because now you'll smooth it all out with a heavy, lightly floured rolling pin.

🍪 Bake 30 to 35 minutes, or until the cake is firm and brown.

🍪 Cool cake for about 5 minutes. You need to work rapidly because when the gingerbread is cold it is almost like concrete!

🍪 While the cake is still warm and still in the pan, lay the cardboard patterns on the baked gingerbread and cut around patterns with a sharp knife. Cut all the way through cake to the pan bottom. Let cake cool completely then lift out the pieces.

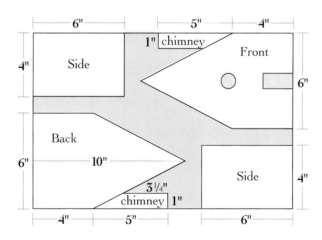

🍪 Prepare second pan of gingerbread. Cut into the following pieces:

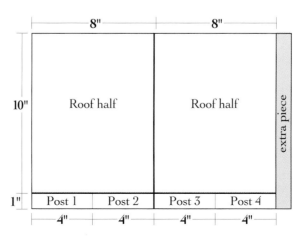

🍪 Prepare third pan of gingerbread. Cut into the following:

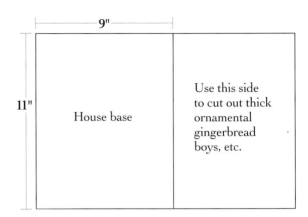

9"

11"

House base

Use this side to cut out thick ornamental gingerbread boys, etc.

Method for decorating the house:

🍪 Prepare the ornamental frosting (recipe follows).

🍪 With pieces of gingerbread still spread out flat, decorate the side walls with windows. Decorate the door and door opening at this time also. Press hard candies into the soft frosting and decorate as you wish. Allow this frosting on windows, door, and door frame to harden completely before actually assembling the house.

🍪 First step in assembling house is to lay the large base piece on a cutting board or a large flat tray. If you wish to "landscape" the house, be sure the board or tray is large enough to add trees and shrubbery. I use an 18" x 24" piece of ½" plywood.

🍪 Using the ornamental frosting as cement, spread it on the bottom edge of one of the side walls of the house, and on the bottom and side edge of one of the end walls. Fit the 2 pieces together on the base and hold 3 or 4 minutes, or until frosting is set.

🍪 Cement a post in the inside corner to support the 2 walls. Allow frosting to set.

🍪 Repeat with remaining side wall and end wall. Cement in remaining supporting posts. Allow frosting to set at least 10 minutes before adding the roof.

🍪 Cement half the roof at a time. Spread frosting on top edges of side and end walls and put roof half in place. Hold in place until frosting sets (this is important — roof half will slide off if frosting isn't set).

🍪 Repeat with the other roof half. Roof tops should meet, but not overlap. Fill the space between with frosting to make the roof peak.

🍪 Cement the 2 chimney pieces together. When set, cement chimney to the roof. (Check photo often to see spacing.)

🍪 When all the frosting is completely set, frost the chimney and roof top.

- Press hard candies into the roof halves while frosting is still moist. Press red hot candies or other small hard candies, into the chimney. Variation: Or, you may let roof frosting harden and attach the candies with dabs of frosting on the back of each candy. Place candy where you want it on the roof and hold for a few seconds to set.

- Cover the base around the house with frosting to look like snow. If you're "landscaping," you need to have trees and shrubbery made and ready to push into the soft frosting at this point.

To achieve the look of snow I want (in other words, plenty of snow), I make at least 3 batches of the ornamental frosting. One batch spreads out too thin, so have plenty of ingredients on hand when you begin the decorating process. If you are decorating the house only, without "landscaping," 1 batch should be enough.

Ornamental Frosting*

Each recipe makes about $3^1/_2$ cups.

4 eggs whites, at room temperature
5 cups confectioners' sugar, sifted

- In a large bowl of an electric mixer, beat egg whites at high speed until stiff, but not dry.

- Gradually add 2 cups of the sugar.

- Reduce speed to medium and gradually add the remaining sugar, frequently scraping down the sides of the bowl with a rubber spatula.

- Beat at high speed for 7 to 8 minutes or until frosting forms **very** stiff peaks.

After frosting is made, you **must** keep the bowl covered with a damp cloth to prevent it from hardening. When it sets up, it truly is like concrete!

Following is the recipe for shrubbery that I make. Each recipe will make 10 or 12 small shrubs (like the ones near the door and around the windows in the photo). So, to make larger trees or shrubs, you may need to make 2, 3 or even more recipes. The "bare trees" in the photo are branches I've picked up in the yard and sprayed white so they'll look snow-covered.

*from *Foods of the World Recipes: The Cooking of Germany © 1969 Time-Life Books, Inc.* Used with permission.

Peppermint Trees and Shrubs

$^2/_3$ cup sugar
$^2/_3$ cup light corn syrup
$^1/_2$ teaspoon salt
$^1/_2$ teaspoon peppermint extract, optional
    green food coloring
4 cups puffed rice cereal, plain, not frosted
    light corn syrup, for decorations
    grated coconut, for decorations

Combine sugar, corn syrup, salt and extract in a large saucepan.

Tint a delicate green with food coloring, or add the coloring drop by drop until you get the desired shade of green.

Heat slowly, stirring constantly, just until sugar dissolves. Remove from heat.

Stir in the cereal. Toss with a wooden spoon until cereal is evenly coated.

Return pan to heat and cook, stirring constantly, over medium heat for 5 minutes, or until mixture is very sticky.

Spray a large sheet of waxed paper or foil with nonstick cooking spray and turn the hot cereal mixture out onto it. Let cool a few minutes until mixture is cool enough to handle.

Lightly grease your hands and while mixture is still warm, shape into shrubs or pyramid-shaped trees. Be careful — this mixture is very hot.

Set each shrub or tree on greased waxed paper to dry.

If you want the shrubs or trees to look snowy, brush each cooled shrub very lightly with slightly warmed light corn syrup and sprinkle grated coconut on top and down sides of each.

When the Holidays are over, we place our house in a large box. Cover the house with tissue paper and store the box in a cool, dry place. After 2 or 3 years, if I find the ornamental frosting is beginning to look yellow, then it's time to make a new house.

You are now the proud owner of a gingerbread house — valuable real estate indeed considering the time spent to assemble, make and decorate it! (I count on parts of 2 or 3 days to complete the project.) But what a wonderfully satisfying project! Be sure to display the house in a very prominent place and expect lots of "oohs," "ahs," and other good comments. Your children and grandchildren will think you're terribly clever!

Christmas Potpourri

Do you ever do something over and over until you get it just right? I have been making this Christmas potpourri for many years and I think I have finally gotten it just right! It is stunningly beautiful with its dark green evergreen pieces, jewel-like orange slices, tiny cones, bright red dried globe amaranth blooms and fragrant whole spices. Add a fragrant oil and here is a potpourri that will take you through the Holidays and beyond.

   Christmas potpourri is very easy to prepare and very inexpensive also. Many of the ingredients come from the yard or garden. A crock or bowl of it makes a splendid gift for someone on your list. I can't think of anyone who wouldn't like some!

Christmas Potpourri *(continued)*

I'll list the ingredients in the potpourri pictured here. If all these things aren't available, substitute beautiful native evergreens, dried flowers, etc., from your area. The key word here is "beautiful." I have long said that a potpourri (any potpourri) is only as pretty as what goes into it.

1. SHORT PIECES OF FRESH EVERGREENS — I use a mixture of junipers, cedars, spruce and arborvitae. Do not select yews as they dry brown. The evergreen sprigs will dry naturally in the potpourri.

2. HEMLOCK CONES — A friend gathers these cones for me from a large tree in her yard. The cones are small and have a rich brown color. If hemlock cones aren't available, choose any small- to medium-sized pine cones.

3. SWEET GUM BALLS — My twin sister, Martha, has lived in the South for many years. They had sweet gum trees in their yard at one of their houses and she introduced me to this beautiful dark brown and spiny cone-like ball. She says it's no fun going barefoot in their yard, but otherwise the sweet gum tree is a beauty. If you don't have them where you live, toss in another handful of pine cones.

4. DRIED APPLE AND ORANGE SLICES — These are most beautiful if dried in a food dehydrator (follow your dehydrator instructions for drying each fruit).

5. DRIED SMALL POMEGRANATES — Sometime around Thanksgiving I buy 4 or 5 pomegranates at the grocery. I look for small, unblemished ones. I lay them in a flat basket and let them dry naturally for several days — it may actually take several weeks for them to completely dry, but they don't need to be that dry to add to this potpourri.

6. DRIED RED GLOBE AMARANTH BLOOMS — The globe amaranth is a great little annual plant for your garden. It starts blooming in June and continues until a hard frost. Keep the blooms picked off and they'll continue to set new blooms. Dry the blooms on their stems tied upside down in a small bundle (strip green leaves off first). When dry, snip the bloom heads off and save for potpourri.

7. WHOLE SPICES — The spices I use are whole allspice, star anise, broken cinnamon sticks, whole nutmeg pieces, whole cloves and vanilla bean pieces.

8. DRIED ORANGE OR LEMON PEEL — Notice the dried orange peel in the photo. Look in a kitchen shop or a gourmet food shop for a small kitchen tool used to strip peel from oranges, lemons, or other citrus fruits. Take a navel orange and with this tool, carefully peel a long strip going around and around the orange. Lay these long strips on a paper plate and let them air dry for a couple of days. They will dry twisted and curled. I like to lay one or two of these strips on top of the potpourri. Don't try to mix it into the potpourri because the strips are brittle when dried and they will break easily.

9. THE FIXATIVE — There are many fixatives that can be used. I use either oak moss, large cut orris root, or frankincense tears (more about this in Christmas Legends, page 99). If I use cinnamon oil for my essential oil, then I use broken cinnamon sticks for my fixative. Think of a fixative as the vehicle to hold the aroma (the essential oil).

10. ESSENTIAL OIL — I usually don't mix oils for this potpourri. I love the singular aroma of cinnamon oil, for example. Another time, I might use pine oil, or balsam pine oil, or clove/orange oil. Whichever oil you choose, each one smells like Christmas!

I have no exact measurements for my Christmas potpourri, but to give you an idea . . .

1	gallon fresh evergreen sprigs
1	cup hemlock cones (or other cones)
1	cup sweet gum balls (or more cones)
6	dried apple slices
6	dried orange slices
3	small dried pomegranates
1	cup dried red globe amaranth blooms (or other small dried red blooms)
½	cup mixed whole spices
½	cup fixative (I use frankincense tears if I have them)
20	drops essential oil
	dried orange or lemon peel

Combine the first 8 ingredients in a large bowl.

Place fixative in a small plastic bag. Add drops of essential oil to the fixative. Close bag and shake to mix well.

Now, gently mix the fixative (with the oil added) into the other ingredients.

Place the potpourri in a large crock, bowl, or wooden bowl.

Lay the dried peel on top.

Enjoy this fragrant and beautiful potpourri throughout the Holidays.

If you choose to use a wooden bowl for displaying this potpourri, line the bowl first with clear plastic wrap. This will protect the bowl surface.

When the potpourri loses its aroma, refresh with more fixative and essential oil.

Luscious Lemon Potpourri

I love anything lemon! Anytime of the year! So it isn't too surprising that I would make this potpourri for the Holidays. It is, of course, necessary to grow, dry and preserve the various herbs I have included in this potpourri during the summer or growing season.

The main ingredient in this mixture is dried lemon verbena leaves. Lemon verbena (Aloysia triphylla) is one of my favorite herbs I grow in the garden. This is a great herb to cook with. It adds powerful lemon flavor to whatever it's added to. I stuff a few leaves in a chicken cavity, drizzle a little butter and fresh lemon juice over the outside of the bird, and roast it to a beautiful golden brown — fabulous chicken! Look for the Lemon Verbena Jelly recipe on page 117 — it's our all-time favorite herb jelly. This talk of food is certainly off the subject of potpourri making, but it's important for you to know just how versatile this herb is.

Lemon verbena is a perennial plant, but in Indiana I must treat it as an annual. Our winters fluctuate from the +40s to the -10s and lemon verbena can't survive that.

After the growing season, I'll choose two or three plants to bring indoors. If I can coax one of them through the winter, I consider myself lucky. When I bring it indoors, I prune about half the growth — this is when I get lots of leaves to dry. The remainder of the leaves will probably fall off during the winter, but if I can keep it alive, I'll haul it back outside in early May, feed and water it, and most likely will see new, little green leaves popping out in a few days.

Because I love to cook with this herb and because I add the dried leaves to my potpourri, I grow four or five lemon verbenas each year. I plant most of them in the herb garden, but I always plant one in a big pot for the patio. It's a wonderful plant for container gardening.

For the potpourri, hang stems of lemon verbena upside down to dry. When leaves are dried on the stem, carefully strip them off and store in closed, plastic bags away from heat and light.

Two other favorite plants play a role in this potpourri. Neither has anything to do with lemon or a lemon aroma, but each blends well with the verbena leaves. One of them is love-in-a-mist (Nigella damascena). This annual plant has insignificant blue, white, pink or purple blooms. If these flowers are not cut, they become beautiful balloon-shaped seed pods with a lacy, net-like covering around each pod. I cut the stems with pods and hang them upside down to dry. I clip these pods off the stems and add them to the Luscious Lemon Potpourri. They add great texture to the mixture. Be sure to cut the stems while the pods are still purplish in color.

Another interesting plant produces "cone-like" fruits that I add to this potpourri. These "cones" are from the female hops vine (Humulus lupulus). Yes, this is the plant used in brewing beer and also used in making some medicines. In the summer, wonderful little green "cones" appear on this hardy perennial vine. They look like immature, tiny pine cones. I cut them when they are green and lay them in a flat basket to dry. Because of their color and texture, they are beautiful to add to this potpourri. Hops are grown in the northwest region of the United States, mainly as a brewing ingredient, but I have seen beautiful wreaths and other decorative items made from these "fruits of the vine."

Another addition to this potpourri is flowerets of the hydrangea bloom. When the blooms are still green-tinged and before they have turned snow white, I cut a few blooms for this mixture. Cut stems about a foot long, hang upside down (only one stem so it will dry evenly all around) for about two weeks. When the blooms are dry, cut into flowerets and add them to the potpourri. They add lightness to the mixture, as well as texture.

As you can see, many of these ingredients must be dried throughout the summer. I make this potpourri in the summer, but I also like to store the dried materials so I can make a fresh batch at Christmastime. This potpourri is not bright and gaudy as flower potpourris can be. Instead, it is a beautiful soft green and cream color and looks quite wonderful in a glass or crystal bowl.

Luscious Lemon Potpourri *(continued)*

Following is a list of ingredients for my Luscious Lemon Potpourri. Feel free to include your own interesting additions.

lemon verbena leaves, dried
pieces of lemon peel, dried
lemon grass, dried and cut into 1" pieces
small pine cones (I use hemlock)
whole star anise
love-in-a-mist pods, dried
hops pods, dried
lemon slices, dehydrator dried
hydrangea flowerets, dried
clusters of tallow berries (or substitute)
$\frac{1}{2}$ cup oak moss, as a fixative
20 drops lemon oil, lemon verbena oil, or a combination of the two

There are no exact measurements for this potpourri. Choose your container and fill it accordingly. The main ingredient, of course, is lemon verbena leaves. Add other ingredients (except the fixative and oil) by the handful or cupful. As in other potpourri-making, place the fixative (oak moss in this case) in a plastic bag, add the essential oil, close bag and shake to distribute oil. Now add the fixative and oil to the remainder of ingredients and mix thoroughly, but gently. When the potpourri loses its aroma (and it will if it's in an open container) refresh with more oak moss, or other fixative, and essential oil.

What a beautiful centerpiece for the tea table or for any Holiday party table, for that matter! It is a three-tiered creation of pomander oranges, undecorated oranges, lemons, yellow and red apples, pomegranates, and small red pears. You could quit here and call it beautiful, but add rosemary sprigs and a few fresh flowers in water tubes and a topper of ivy streamers, and it truly becomes spectacular.

A Christmas Topiary of Pomanders, Fruits, Rosemary and Fresh Flowers

I started collecting footed glass cake stands several years ago. Mother gave me my first one and I've slowly added to the collection since. For the topiary in the picture, I chose three cake stands — the bottom one is 14" in diameter, the middle one is 11", and the little one on top is 9". It's best to arrange the fruits, flowers, and herbs on the cake stands in place — when the topiary is completed, it's very heavy.

A Christmas Topiary of Pomanders, Fruits, Rosemary and Fresh Flowers *(continued)*

Let's talk about pomanders before I explain how I put the topiary together. Pomanders are made one of two ways. One way is the old fashioned method of entirely covering an orange with whole cloves, then rolling the orange in a spice and powdered orris root mixture* to preserve the orange. When properly prepared, these pomanders will last for years. Tie a pretty ribbon around one and hang in your closet. You'll notice a gentle spice fragrance each time you open the closet door. These lasting pomanders make nice little gifts.

*Combine:

2	tablespoons ground cinnamon
1	tablespoon ground cloves
1	tablespoon ground allspice
2	tablespoons ground orris root (a fixative)

Mix well and roll the clove-studded orange in this mixture. Gently shake off excess, then lay orange on newspapers or paper towels to cure and dry. Oranges need to dry 2 or more weeks before adding a ribbon. Keep any spice-orris root mixture that is left over in a closed, airtight container. Be sure to mark it well and do not use for cooking purposes.

The second method of making pomanders is cutting strips from the orange peel and inserting whole cloves in those cut out areas. I call these decorative pomanders. Look for a small kitchen tool that is used for this purpose. I don't know what the real name of one is, but I call it a peel stripper. These are available in fancy food shops or shops that carry specialty kitchen items. Hold a navel orange in one hand and peel strips from the orange in various patterns, such as:

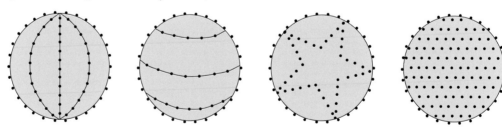

Be sure to save these strips — dry them for making potpourri.

These are beautiful pomanders because much of the orange color shows through, but they are not long-lasting. I make decorative pomanders for a topiary the day before I put the topiary together. I wrap each completed orange in plastic wrap and keep refrigerated until ready to use.

Variation: If you do not have a peel stripper, push whole cloves into the orange rind in the same pattern or patterns illustrated. It's a little more difficult to keep the lines straight, but the orange will last longer since strips have not been removed from the rind.

For the Christmas topiary pictured, I used:

- 3   glass cake stands, 14", 11" and 9" in diameter
- 1   small glass for top tier
- 18   undecorated navel oranges
- 12   decorated pomander oranges
- 12   lemons
- 12   to 15 red apples (I used Red Rome and Gala)
- 12   to 15 yellow apples (Yellow Delicious)
- 18   small red pears
- 12   6" to 8" rosemary sprigs
- 12   stems of white freesias (wonderfully fragrant!)
- 12   stems of yellow freesias (also fragrant)
- 6   pomegranates
      a few extra rosemary sprigs for the top
- 4   12" to 18" trailing ivy vines
- 24   short water tubes (available from the florist)

Put the stands in place on your table or sideboard.

Set the small glass filled with water in the middle of the top tier.

Start piling the undecorated oranges, lemons, apples and pomegranates onto each tier in a random fashion.

Place the pomander oranges so they are prominently displayed.

Insert rosemary sprigs and freesias into filled water tubes and push them in among the fruits so that the tubes don't show.

Fill in spaces with the small red pears.

Put rosemary sprigs in the glass on top and add the 4 ivy vines (check photo).

If desired, add Christmas greenery and perhaps a ribbon or bow at the base of the topiary. This is too beautiful not to share with family and friends!

Variations:
1. For other times of the year, omit the pomander oranges and add other fruits such as little bunches of grapes, big Bing cherries, large strawberries with green stems still attached, nectarines, etc. . . Use whatever fruit is seasonal or looks beautiful at the grocery or market.
2. The flowers and herbs you could choose are endless! Geranium blooms, small tulip blooms, roses, lilies, even zinnias and marigolds are all beautiful choices for a topiary. Rosemary, sage, thyme, oregano, mints, French tarragon and many more — all would be fragrant and beautiful to use in a topiary.
3. Use long, thin strips of orange or lemon peel to drape over and down the sides of the top tier. Another time, use beautiful, narrow satin ribbon streamers to match your color scheme.

Imagine this — purple Japanese iris, lemons, lemon thyme sprigs — nothing else — arranged as a topiary. It's beautiful.

Use your imagination and create!

Christmas Legends

Webster says a legend is, "A story or account, nonhistorical or unverifiable, which is handed down by tradition from earlier times and popularly accepted as factual." The following Christmas legends certainly fit this definition. We have heard of these stories since childhood and, in fact, they have become real to us. In my mind, I have no doubt, for example, that the Baby was laid in a manger with certain herbs added to the bedding.

I'm not asking you to believe these legends — just imagine that they could have taken place. Believe them or not, they make great stories to pass on to our children. I've collected this material over the years. Notice that most of this material deals with herbs and spices. At this point in the book, this shouldn't surprise you!

THE CHRISTMAS ROSE

The Christmas rose (*Helleborous Niger*) is a poisonous wintergreen herb. It blooms at Christmastime in moderate climates. Legend has it that the flowers of the rose were originally black (niger means black), but turned snow white to honor the birth of Christ. In early Christian days, the flowers were symbols of purity and humility.

ROSEMARY

Of all the herbs, rosemary (*Rosmarinus officinalis*) is considered by many to be the Christmas herb. Rosemary is the herb of remembrance and fidelity and was thought to be one of the manger herbs. As you will see on previous pages of this book, I use rosemary many ways at Christmastime. Its wonderful pine-like scent mingles with other Christmas aromas — it belongs with Christmas.

There are other legends about rosemary too interesting not to mention, even though they don't deal with Christmas. It is a fact that rosemary is a perennial plant native to the Mediterranean area. In its native land, rosemary grows as tall as a hedge. There is a legend that says that rosemary bushes grow to 6 feet tall in 33 years — the stature (height) and life of Christ — but that the plant ceases its vertical growth after 6 feet, so as never to stand taller than He did.

And as I have mentioned earlier, another legend says that the delicate blue flowers that appear on rosemary plants are attributed to the Virgin Mary. As the legend goes, Mary draped her blue cloak over a white-blooming rosemary bush during the flight into Egypt, and the rosemary blooms have had the blue color of her cloak ever since.

GOLD, FRANKINCENSE AND MYRRH

We all know what gold is. It is the same valuable commodity today that it was in Jesus' time. It's hard to believe that tree resins could also be so valuable, but at the time of Jesus' birth, the resins frankincense and myrrh were equally, or even more valuable than gold. I have read that in those early days, gold was equal to $600 per pound, frankincense was equal to $500 per pound, and myrrh was equal to $1,000 per pound! They were considered valuable because of medicinal qualities as well as their aromatic qualities.

Frankincense (*genus Boswellia*) is an aromatic resin, amber in color, and originates from various Asiatic and African trees. It was important medicinally and was (and still is) chiefly used for burning as incense. I have read that frankincense is mentioned 17 times in the Bible — most of those times in the Old Testament. The resin runs down the bark of the tree and dries in "tears" or tear-shaped droplets. I sometimes use these frankincense tears as a fixative in potpourri-making.

Myrrh (*Commiphora myrrha*) was also a valuable resin, actually twice as valuable as frankincense. It is reddish orange in color, from small, unattractive and spiny trees native to Arabia and East Africa. Myrrh is also used medicinally and for incense and perfume-making.

And so when the Wise Men presented the Child with gifts of "gold, frankincense and myrrh," they truly were gifts of great value.

MANGER HERBS

There is a wonderful legend about certain herbs that were used to freshen the manger that Jesus laid in. Those herbs are said to be rosemary, thyme, pennyroyal, our lady's bedstraw and lavender.

Rosemary (*Rosmarinus officinalis*) This tender perennial has already been discussed, but I might add that it would seem very likely that this herb was used in the manger because it is native to the area and because of its soft pine-like and clean aroma.

Thyme (*Thymus vulgaris* or *Thymus serphyllum*) This perennial herb represents bravery of the Holy Child. It grew profusely in the Mediterranean region in Biblical times as well as now. Thyme rather mats together as it grows, so it would have made a nice cushion to lay the Child on. Thyme has a soft spicy-sweet aroma.

Pennyroyal (*Mentha pulegium* or *Hedeoma pulegioides*) Pennyroyal is a perennial used in making medicine and also a very aromatic oil is extracted from it. It is a member of the mint family so, of course, it is very aromatic. It would impart a cool and pungent aroma in the manger.

Our Lady's Bedstraw (*Galium verum*) In Biblical times, people used this herb to stuff their mattresses with, especially birthing bed mattresses. When our lady's bedstraw is dry, it is similar to wheat straw. It is a perennial and a close relative of sweet woodruff.

Lavender (*Lavandul officinalis*) This is the herb of purity and virtue. It is a gray-green perennial that also grows profusely in the Mediterranean area. Lavender is a beautiful herb treasured for its fragrant leaves, flowers and oil. It is said to have been Mary's favorite herb, so it would certainly have been one of the manger herbs.

Biblical Herbs

Besides the herbs already mentioned that are associated with Christmas, there are many other herbs mentioned in the Bible. So what I wish to tell you about Biblical herbs really has nothing to do with Christmas (in most cases), but I just hope you'll find the subject as interesting as I do.

The Holy Land is native to many plants and trees. The climate is temperate and the soil is productive. The Hebrew translation for "herb," by the way, is "green thing."

Herbs are mentioned many, many times in the Bible and by now you know that I have a passion for anything herbal, so what little I have learned on this vast subject is shared on the following pages.

Hyssop (*Hyssopus officinalis*) This herb is a member of the mint family. It is a perennial plant and very hardy. It is actually an evergreen with narrow, dark green leaves so it works well as an edging or low hedge. The Herbrew word for hyssop is "ezob," meaning "holy plant."

I start with hyssop because it is mentioned over and over again in the Bible and was used so many different ways in church or synagogue ceremonies. In Biblical times, it was used to cleanse the body and soul. It was thought to purify people of disease and sin. The so-called bitter herbs, such as hyssop, were eaten by the Jews during Passover as a show of penitence.

Historically, hyssop is known as a holy herb because it was used for cleansing sacred places. In Psalm 51:7, David says in a prayer, "purge me with hyssop and I shall be clean." In John 19:29, hyssop is mentioned at the crucifixion: "There was a vessel full of vinegar and they filled a sponge with the vinegar and put it upon hyssop and put it in His mouth." Throughout the history of the church, hyssop has been known for its cleansing powers. When Westminister Abbey in London was consecrated, hyssop was sprinkled on the altar so that this great cathedral was cleansed before it was used as a place of worship.

Rue (*Ruta graveolens*) This is a hardy perennial herb with clusters of very small yellow flowers and strongly scented gray-green leaves. The aromatic oil from rue is used in certain medicines. It is called the herb of grace and is also sometimes referred to as the herb of repentance.

At one time in the Catholic Church, brushes made of rue were used to sprinkle the holy water at the ceremony preceding High Mass.

Coriander (*Coriandrum sativum*) Though an annual plant, coriander will reseed itself. This is actually a dual herb — the new green growth is called **cilantro**. Cilantro is widely used in Mexican and Eastern cooking. It is an herb added to salsa, for example. If it goes to seed, the dried seed is called **coriander**. Dried coriander seeds smell like sage and lemon combined.

Coriander is a tremendously interesting Bible herb! There are several Old Testament references to coriander as the herb whose fruit (the seeds) is the food (or manna) that God showered on the Israelites during their desert trek from bondage. In Exodus 16:31, 35 it says: "And the house of Israel called the name thereof manna; and it was like coriander seed, white; and the taste of it was like wafers made with honey." (35) "And the children of Israel did eat manna for 40 years, until they came unto the borders of the land of Canaan."!

Costmary (*Chrysanthemum balsamita*) A perennial plant, costmary has very fragrant leaves. It is considered the herb of everlasting life. The plant has large, flat leaves that have a sweet mint fragrance. Costmary is supposedly the herb that Mary Magdalene used to make her ointments with. In our colonial times, the herb was referred to as "Bible leaf herb" because the colonists used the leaves for bookmarks in their Bibles. Costmary is also used for medicinal purposes, even today.

Wormwood (*Artemisia absinthium*) This herb is also an interesting Bible herb. Like hyssop, wormwood is a bitter herb. It is fine-leafed, very pretty and a very hardy perennial plant. It is in the artemisia family — common dusty miller and French tarragon are also members. Wormwood is toxic and should not be taken internally. It is, however, the chief ingredient in a liqueur called **Absinthe**. This liqueur is so mind-altering that it is illegal to sell!

Wormwood is referred to in the Bible in Revelations 8:10, 11: "And the third angel sounded, and there fell a great star from heaven; burning as it were a lamp, and it fell upon the third part of the rivers, and upon the fountains of waters; (11) And the name of the star is wormwood; and the third part of the waters became wormwood; and many men died of the waters, because they were made bitter."

Chervil (*Anthriscus cerefolium*) Chervil is a hardy annual that grows about 12" tall. It is one of the traditional ingredients in the French herbal mixture called fines herbes. It has become an important culinary herb because of its delicate parsley taste. The herb is said to have great qualities of rejuvenation. In Europe, people eat chervil on Holy Thursday (Maundy Thursday) as a symbol of resurrection and new life. Chervil's aroma is likened to the aroma of myrrh and it is sometimes called myrrhis.

Anise, Mint and Cumin — Anise (*Pimpinella anisum*), mint (*Mentha*) and cumin (*Cuminum cyminum*) are mentioned together here because I found a reference to all three of them in Matthew 23:23: "Woe unto you, scribes and Pharisees, hypocrites! for ye pay tithes of mint, anise and cumin, and have omitted weightier matters of the law, judgment, mercy and faith." So, these herbs were actually used as commodities to pay taxes with! Try that today and see where it would get you!

Anise is an annual plant that has been known of and used for centuries. Colonists brought aniseed to North America and it became popular with the Shakers. They grew it as a medicinal crop. The seed is also used in baking and I sometimes add seeds to my potpourri. The leaves have a faint licorice taste and are good chopped into fruit salads.

There are so many varieties of **mint**, a perennial, and so many ways to use them that I can't begin to name them all here. Centuries ago, the Hebrews laid mint on synagogue floors. The air was perfumed with mint as worshippers walked across the floor. Hundreds of years later, the Italians repeated the old practice in their churches where the herb is called **Erba Santa Maria.** There are many culinary, cosmetic and medicinal uses of the mints.

Cumin is a tender annual only a few inches tall. The cumin seeds are similar in appearance to caraway seed, except they are rather hairy. The seeds are very pungent and are used in food preparation, liqueurs, cosmetics, perfumes and also in medicines.

Calendula (*Calendula officinalis*) This is also referred to as pot marigold. Calendula is a hardy annual that grows from one to two feet tall. It flowers almost continuously with bright yellow blooms. The flowers are used in cosmetics and in culinary recipes. It is also used as a dye plant and is known for its many healing properties. Europeans have long used calendula petals to flavor soups and to color butter and cheeses.

Calendula is also associated with the Virgin Mary because she supposedly wore golden blossoms on her cloak. The monks named the golden flowers "Mary Gowles"; hence our marigolds!

Dogwood (*Cornus florida*) The dogwood is an ornamental tree but its bark, flowers and fruit are used in certain medicines. It is documented that during the American Civil War, dogwood bark provided a substitute for quinine when it was not available. You will find a dogwood tree in most Biblical herb gardens, and most certainly it can be found in church or cathedral gardens.

Legend has it that when Christ was crucified, the dogwood was the size of an oak tree! It was such a sturdy tree, the dogwood was chosen as the timber for the cross (according to the legend). The use of the tree for a cross made the tree so sad that Jesus said the dogwood would never again grow large enough to be used as a cross. He said that in the future, it would be slender, bent and twisted. He also said its blossoms would be in the shape of a cross with the print of the crucifixion nails in each petal. In the center of the flower would be the crown of thorns. Jesus said the dogwood tree would not be destroyed — it was to be cherished as a reminder of His death on the cross.

Basil (*Ocimum basilicum*) Basil is such an important culinary herb, but it also played a role in early Christianity. It is said that basil grew around Christ's tomb after the resurrection. Many churches, even today, place pots of basil near the altar, especially at Easter time.

Angelica (*Angelica Archangelica*) I'm not sure this herb is mentioned in the Bible, but with a name like this it should be! Angelica is a large biennial plant growing to five feet tall with very large aromatic leaves. The stems of this herb can be candied for adding to fruitcakes. It is said to have gotten its name because it bloomed on the feast day of the Archangel Michael. It was a gift from the angels to protect people from the plague and also from evil.

Horehound (*Marrubium vulgare*) Horehound is a hardy perennial that is best known for its medicinal qualities. This herb extract is used to make cough drops and it's also popular as a flavoring in candy. Long ago, it was thought to cure many illnesses. **Marrubinum** comes from the Hebrew word **marrob** which means bitter. It is used even today as one of the bitter herbs in the Passover seder.

Tansy (*Tanacetum vulgare*) Tansy is a very hardy perennial that needs to be watched so it doesn't overspread your garden or herbal border. Tansy has strong antiseptic properties and has been used as an insecticide and a disinfectant. It was used as a strewing herb in ancient times. At one time, tansy was added to meats and egg dishes for flavor. It is not used today as a culinary herb - it is potentially toxic. Tansy is found in old monastery gardens as well as modern gardens. The small yellow flowers of the tansy dry nicely for dried flower arrangements.

Flax (*Linum usitatissimum*) An ancient herb, flax is an annual that grows one to three feet tall. It is a very useful plant. The oil from flax seed is called linseed oil and is used in paint manufacturing. The stems are processed to make paper and, of course, the beautiful fabric we call linen is made from flax. Flax is refereed to in the Bible in Genesis 41:42 - Pharaoh dresses Joseph in linen and gold to aid him in interpreting his dream. Flax and linen are referred to several other times in the Bible, but perhaps the most significant reference is at the time of Jesus' death. His burial shroud was made of linen and it was this cloth that was left in the tomb at the resurrection (John 20:5-7).

Lady's Mantle (*Alchemilla vulgaris*) This lovely plant derives its common name from its leaves that are "pleated" to look somewhat like a lady's cloak. It is a hardy perennial (may need mulching in cold climates) with tiny yellow flowers. This herb has a great reputation as a healing agent. In ancient times, the alchemists used the drops of dew that collected on the leaves in their potions. The leaves are used today in making many medicines. This is a beautiful low growing border plant for the herb garden.

Balm of Gilead (*commiphora opobalsamum*) This is the true plant that yields the balm (oil) mentioned in Ezekiel 27:17. The plant referred to in Ezekiel is a very rare shrub of the desert. You're not likely to find a true Balm of Gilead shrub in an herb garden because it is illegal to export the shrub from its native land. Another shrub with similar properties is also called Balm of Gilead (*cedronella canariensi*). The leaves have a musky scent which makes it popular in the production of men's fragrances. This is a nice plant for a container because it grows three or four feet tall.

Borage (*Borago officinalis*) I cannot document that borage is a Biblical herb. I mention it because the plant produces the most beautiful blue flowers. Long ago, many Flemish old masters painted the Virgin Mary's robe the blue color of the borage plant's bloom. Today it is a lovely two to three feet tall annual plant grown mainly for its edible flowers. Sometimes I candy the blooms - they are beautiful to dress up desserts. The leaves have a faint cucumber scent and taste - some cooks chop the young leaves into green salads.

Madonna Lily (*Lilium candidum*) This very old plant is known for its stark white and intensely fragrant bloom. Catholic artists called it the Madonna lily because they dedicated its purity and whiteness to the Virgin Mary. It says in Hosea 14:5: "I will be as the dew to Israel; he shall blossom as the lily." This wonderful old plant will grow four or five feet tall, likes a sunny location, and will come back year after year in the garden. If you can find the bulbs, these lilies should definitely be planted in a Biblical herb garden.

Crown of Thorns (*Paliurus* or *Ziziphus*) These two species of shrubs were common in the Holy Land in Biblical days. Both of these shrubs are referred to as Christ's crown of thorns and one of them was probably the shrub that the Roman soldiers made the crown from. You can read about this in Matthew 27:29 and John 19:2. I'm not sure these are considered herb plants, but they are certainly Biblical plants.

Chicory (*Cichorium intybus*) The more I read and learn about herbs, the more fascinated I become with this broad subject! Chicory is one of these fascinating herbs! It is a tall hardy perennial with many uses. Leaves of the chicory are one of the bitter herbs modern Jews eat to celebrate the Passover meal. If you dig the roots of the chicory plant, cut off the top green growth, bury these roots in a sandy compost, water them but don't give them any light, in three or four weeks you can harvest chicons, or Belgian endive! Considering how expensive Belgian endive is, this would be a good project. Last, but not least, the roots of the chicory can be cut, dried and roasted, then added to coffee. What a versatile herb!

As you can see, many of the herbs we use every day are derived from plants that grew centuries ago.

The Best Gift
is a
Homemade
Gift

The Best Gift is a Homemade Gift

How true this is! Some of you are going to say, but I don't have time to make homemade gifts! Well, that's true I'm sure for some of us, but if you took one of those long, tiring days of Christmas shopping and spent it in your kitchen instead, you would be surprised how many of the following gift ideas you could complete in just that one day!

Many of the recipes can and should be prepared several days, or even weeks, ahead of time. The breads, cakes and most of the cookies can all be made in advance, wrapped well and frozen. The flavored vinegars, fruited wines and liqueurs must be made in November or early December to develop the best flavors. Some of the special jellies can be made in late summer or early fall. And what fun it would be to plan a day to make Christmas ornaments! So, take some of the drudgery out of gift shopping and spend an enjoyable day at home creating gifts that will greatly please those on your list.

The gift, of course, is important, but how the gift is presented is also important. The bottle, jar, or container that the gift comes in is actually a part of the gift, so give some thought to packaging.

Look for interesting old boxes, tins, bottles, mugs, cups and saucers, and tea pots at garage or yard sales, flea markets, antiques shops, or from your own cupboard shelves. These make great containers for cookies, cakes, vinegars or liqueurs. The mugs, cups and saucers or tea pots are wonderful containers for your gifts of flavored coffees or herbal teas.

The contents of flavored vinegar bottles can give you an idea how to decorate that container. For example, tie a raffia bow on a bottle of herbed white wine vinegar. Add a little bunch of herbs and glue two or three cloves of garlic to

continued

the bow with a hot glue gun.

Cover jelly jar tops with fabric or wallpaper remnants. Put a ribbon around the jar lid or add a bow to the top for a pretty package.

Make a loaf of homemade bread a special gift by wrapping the loaf first in plastic wrap, then wrap in a pretty tea or kitchen towel. Add a big bow and you have a beautiful and delicious gift for someone special. Cut strips of fabric, even scraps of silk, with pinking shears and use those strips as ribbon. You can cut your "ribbons" as narrow or as wide as you wish.

If you have a hot glue gun (I couldn't get along without one!), use it to attach small dried berries, nuts still in their shells, rose hips, dried apple slices, dried orange slices, whole spices such as cinnamon sticks and star anise to your bottles or packages.

One of the prettiest gifts I give is a bottle of Cranberry Wine (see page 111). I tie a green grosgrain ribbon around the neck and add a little wreath of cranberries I have sewed together. I keep a large-eyed darning needle and heavy thread handy to make little wreaths to drape over bottle necks. Because this wine should be kept refrigerated, the cranberry wreath will last a long time.

Be on the lookout through the year for interesting and often inexpensive items to make your homemade gift even more special.

The following recipes were chosen partly because of their ease of preparation, but mainly because each is superb. Any one of them would be a thoughtful and welcome gift.

As much as possible, the recipes will coincide with the pictures from top, left to right. In other words, after the first picture, the first recipe is for Homemade Galliano.

Top, left to right: Homemade Galliano, Simmering Citrus Potpourri, Apple Brandy, Cranberry Wine, Cranberry Conserve, Dill Garlic Vinegar, Purple Ruffles Basil Vinegar, Cranberry Orange Butter, Lemon Verbena Jelly, Marie Wallace's World's Best Cookies, Cherry Coconut Bars. Not pictured: Herb Jelly, Cinnamon Honey Butter, Herb Butters.

Homemade Galliano

This great licorice-tasting liqueur is so like the real thing from Italy, only a connoisseur could tell the difference!

4	cups sugar
1	750 ml. bottle filled with hot water
1	750 ml. bottle 190 proof grain alcohol
12	drops anise oil*
8	drops almond extract*
6	drops orange extract*
10	drops yellow food coloring

Pour water into a large bowl. Add sugar and stir to dissolve. Let cool to room temperature. Add the alcohol and stir. Now stir in the oil and extracts, one at a time. Add food coloring and stir. Pour into a large glass container. Cover tightly and store at room temperature for 2 weeks. Sterilize 2 bottles or decanters. Fit a coffee filter into a small funnel and filter the contents of the glass container into the sterilized bottles. This makes about 2 (750 ml.) bottles of delicious liqueur.

* Use only the best quality oil and extracts for this recipe.

Simmering Citrus Potpourri

Combine the following: **1 cup dried orange peel***, cut up, **½ cup dried lemon peel***, cut up, **½ cup cinnamon stick pieces**, **½ cup whole allspice**, **¼ cup whole cloves**, **¼ cup anise seed**, **1 to 2 tablespoons coriander seed** (optional), **½ cup bay leaves** and **1 teaspoon orange oil.**
    Combine dried peels and other ingredients and mix well. Put mixture in an airtight container. To use, combine **1 cup water** with **3 tablespoons potpourri** in a pan or potpourri burner. Simmer and enjoy.

* Dry peels 1 of 3 ways: 1) Lay pieces on paper plates. Cover with a paper towel and let them dry naturally for 3 or 4 days, or until peels are dry. 2) Dry on a microwave-safe plate, covered with paper towels, in your microwave on high. Start with 1 minute, rotate plate, microwave another minute and check to see if peels are dry. Continue drying, but do not brown. 3) Dry in food dehydrator. Pieces will take 2 or 3 hours, more or less.

Apple Brandy

What a great gift! I make 2 or 3 batches of this each year — one batch for us and one or two to give away. I have had people return the empty bottle and ask for a refill — that should give you an idea just how good this is!

4	cups Granny Smith apples, coarsely chopped
1	cup sugar
4	sticks cinnamon, broken
2	cups unflavored brandy

Combine all ingredients in a large sterilized glass jar. Stir to dissolve the sugar. Put a lid on the jar. Once each day for 4 or 5 days, turn jar upside down and shake. Store in a cool, dark place 4 to 6 weeks. Discard apple and cinnamon pieces and strain brandy through several layers of cheesecloth* into sterilized bottles. Cork and label. Each recipe makes about 3 cups.

* I use cheesecloth here instead of a coffee filter because this flavored brandy is rather thick so will not easily drain through a coffee filter. After filtering through the cheesecloth, if desired, then filter the brandy through a coffee filter — you'll now have a beautiful and clear brandy.

Cranberry Wine

*Unbelievably good. It's also very beautiful. You **must** keep a bottle for yourself to serve on Christmas Eve!*

3	cups cranberries, picked over and washed
3	cups sugar
3	750 ml. bottles good dry white wine

Place clean cranberries in your food processor and process only until chopped rather coarse — do not overprocess. Combine cranberries and sugar in a large glass jar. Slowly add the wine and stir as you pour. Stir until sugar is completely dissolved. Cover the jar with plastic wrap and secure with a rubber band. Store jar in the refrigerator for 3 weeks to develop flavor.

After 3 weeks, strain the wine through cheesecloth and discard the cranberries. Strain again through a coffee filter (fitted into a funnel) into sterilized glass bottles. Cork and label. Be sure to tell your friends to keep the bottles refrigerated and any unused portion refrigerated.

Cranberry Conserve

Like the Fabulous Pecan Bars, this recipe is so good it needs to be printed again. It is simply the best cranberry "relish" I know of. When my recipe was published a few years ago in a farm magazine's Christmas article, I received nearly 600 letters with comments about this recipe! Unbelievable! Many women wrote saying the conserve was among the favorite gifts they had given that Christmas.

I use this conserve to accompany chicken, turkey or pork. Sometimes I fill a peach or pear half with a tablespoonful. I glaze chicken breasts with it, then bake the breasts. I've glazed pork roasts with it. I've even brushed it on the turkey the last few minutes of baking time for a beautiful finish to the bird. I'm very sure you will find favorite ways to use it also. Enjoy! And make plenty!

4	cups raw cranberries, picked over and washed
1½	cups water
3	cups sugar
1	cup crushed pineapple, undrained
½	cup light raisins
1	seedless orange, chopped (including the rind)
½	cup walnuts or pecans, chopped

In a large, heavy saucepan, combine the cranberries and water. Bring to a boil over medium heat and simmer for 5 to 8 minutes, or until berries pop and are tender.
Stir in the sugar, crushed pineapple, raisins and chopped orange.
Bring mixture to a boil, reduce heat and simmer for 20 minutes, stirring occasionally. Remove from heat and stir in the nuts.
Can in hot, sterilized jars or cool and store in the refrigerator if conserve is to be used soon.
Makes about 5 cups.

PERFECT.

Flavored Vinegars

Much has been written about "flavored" vinegars and still many of us don't take advantage of using them. They are relatively easy to make and once you're used to cooking with them, you'll find the food you've added them to is pretty drab without them.

I hear people talking about "making" herbal vinegars. Well, in most cases, they really aren't "making" the vinegar, they are adding flavor (herbs, spices, fruits, for example) to store-bought vinegar. So, hopefully, the following will help you understand just how easy it is to develop some of those wonderful flavors.

There are a few basic rules of vinegar flavoring. One is the vinegar you choose. I usually use white distilled (5% acidic) because of the clear colors I get (for example, purple ruffles basil in white distilled vinegar makes a brilliant red product; whereas, the same purple ruffles basil in cider vinegar (which is golden brown) will not produce the same brilliant color — it may taste as good, but it won't look the same). This is not to say you should use only white distilled vinegar. Experiment with white wine vinegar, red wine vinegar, cider vinegar and even rice wine vinegar. They will all produce a good product, but the same herb in each vinegar will make a different looking and tasting vinegar.

Another rule to follow in flavoring vinegar is to use enough of the flavoring material to produce a robust flavor. For example, don't expect a brilliant red vinegar if you use only a handful of purple ruffles basil leaves and stems to a gallon of vinegar! I fill sterilized glass or plastic gallon jars with clean, dry leaves and tender stems, gently pack them into the jar, and pour hot or cold vinegar over them. I usually use cold vinegar right out of the jug. Cover jar or container (use **no** metal), store in a cool, dark place for four weeks or so. After this time, throw away the leaves (or other flavoring agents), strain vinegar into pretty, sterilized bottles and cork or seal. By the way, I usually don't put sprigs of herbs in the final product. The herb will wilt and lose most of its color and I don't think the addition enhances the look of the finished vinegar — however, this is only my preference. It's certainly permissible to add clean, dry herb sprigs to your bottles if you prefer.

Many of my "herbal" friends make their vinegars by setting the bottles in sunny windows or even in the garden (where they would get lots of sun). If that works for them or you, that's fine — I like the slow, cool, dark process of drawing out the color and flavor. It's all a personal preference.

continued

I use a coffee filter fitted into a small funnel to transfer the vinegar from the large container into the bottle.

Flavored vinegars have many uses. Generally, wherever vinegars are used, a flavored vinegar can be substituted with great success. I've listed several ways to use them:

1. salad dressings
2. meat marinades
3. splash on cold cooked vegetables
4. marinate olives, roasted pepper strips and other salad ingredients
5. splash the fruited vinegars or minted vinegars on fresh strawberries or other fruits
6. add to mayonnaise or other cooked dressings to add to salads (about 1 tablespoon vinegar to 1 cup of mayonnaise)
7. de-glaze the frying pan
8. add to tartar sauce to zip up fish dishes

Don't be afraid to use these vinegars wherever you need a burst of flavor!

Look for the following vinegar recipes through the gift section — Dill Garlic Vinegar, Purple Ruffles Basil Vinegar, Raspberry Vinegar, Strawberry Vinegar and Herbed White Wine Vinegar. Two are made with white distilled vinegar, two with white wine vinegar, and one with red wine vinegar. One or more of these vinegars would make a fabulous gift.

Dill Garlic Vinegar

This is a nice vinegar to make in the winter because it uses dried herbs. Add a tablespoon or two of this vinegar to the next potato salad you make — you'll be amazed at the wonderful dill flavor. Marinate cucumber and onion slices in some of this vinegar for a cold and delicious salad. Dill vinegar is superb with fish dishes, especially salmon.

1	quart white distilled vinegar
1	tablespoon dried dill weed
1	tablespoon dried dill seed
4	or 5 cloves of garlic, peeled and coarsely chopped

Sterilize a glass quart jar. Heat the vinegar to nearly the boiling point. Place the dill weed, dill seed and garlic pieces into the jar. Add the hot vinegar to the jar. Cover the jar with a glass lid or plastic wrap — do not use metal. Let steep 2 or 3 weeks to develop flavors. Strain out the herbs and garlic, and throw them away. Fit a coffee filter into a funnel and strain vinegar into a sterilized, pretty jar or bottle. Cork, label, and add a bow and you have a beautiful gift for yourself or a friend. Makes 1 quart.

Purple Ruffles Basil Vinegar

In my opinion, this is the best flavored vinegar of all I have tasted or made. It is incredibly beautiful and one whiff or taste takes you back to the herb garden on a summer day when the garden is at its best. This is such a basic recipe, I nearly didn't include it, but a friend urged me to write down exactly how it's made so that she, as well as you, could successfully make it also. After I tell you how I make the vinegar, I'll give you a recipe for the easiest, fastest and one of the best salad dressings I make.

- 1   sterilized glass (or plastic) gallon jar
       fresh purple ruffles basil leaves and tender stems to fill the jar
- 1   gallon (5% acidic) white distilled vinegar

Gather the purple ruffles basil and bring to the kitchen. Swish the stems and leaves in a pan of tepid water to clean them. Shake off excess water and spread the basil on towels to dry. This will take 2 or 3 hours. The leaves may wilt a little during this time, but that's okay. Put leaves and tender stems into the glass container to nearly fill it. Don't pack them in, but you do need plenty of plant material to make the tastiest and most fragrant vinegar. Now pour a gallon of white distilled vinegar over the herbs. (You may not be able to use quite all the gallon.) I do not heat the vinegar for this recipe. Put a nonmetallic lid on the jar and store in a cool, dark place for about 4 weeks to develop the color and flavor. If I don't have a lid that fits, I place several layers of plastic wrap over the jar opening and secure it with a rubber band — this works fine. After 4 weeks, remove the herbs and discard them. Fit a coffee filter into a small funnel and filter the vinegar from the jar into sterilized bottles. Cork, label and enjoy! Now for the salad dressing....

- 1   package Good Seasons Italian or Garlic Herb dressing mix
- 1/4   cup plus 2 tablespoons purple ruffles basil vinegar
- 1/2   cup salad oil

Combine contents of the mix and the vinegar. Mix well. Add oil and whisk. Note that I don't use water in the dressing, only vinegar. Besides dressing a green salad, drizzle this dressing over tomato slices.

     If you can bear to part with any, this vinegar makes a fabulous gift.

Flavored Butters

*I*t's easy to see why flavored butters have become an important seasoning to use in cooking. I like to compare flavored butters with herbal vinegars — each (butter and vinegar) is wonderful alone, but add spices, herbs, or other seasonings and these stand-by staples become something special. If your children or grandchildren like to sprinkle cinnamon and sugar on their toast, imagine how they would like Cinnamon Honey Butter instead. When I serve tea in the afternoon at Holiday time, I never serve plain butter with the biscuits or scones, I serve a butter such as the Cranberry Orange Butter which is loaded with flavor. Think of additions you can make to butter to add interest and flavor to whatever you're cooking — you'll become a better cook because of it! By the way, if you can't or shouldn't use butter, buy the best brand of margarine as a substitute.

If fresh herbs aren't available to you at Holiday time, then try a butter recipe with dried herbs. Some suggested uses for fresh or dried herb butters are:

1. spread on bread for a roast beef, chicken, or turkey sandwich
2. dress a baked potato
3. use in your white or cheese sauces in place of plain butter
4. season vegetables
5. rub inside and outside of a turkey or chicken to roast
6. dab on fish or chicken to broil

Use your imagination and don't be afraid to experiment!

Cranberry Orange Butter

Terrific on hot biscuits or rolls. Melt some of the mixture and baste a roasting chicken with it — puts a beautiful glaze on the bird.

    1   cup butter
    1/3 cup whole cranberry sauce, or Cranberry Compote (see page 113)
    2   tablespoons orange marmalade

Place butter in a small mixing bowl and beat on high until butter is light and fluffy. Reduce speed and gradually add the cranberry sauce and the marmalade. Mix well. Cover and store for up to 3 weeks in the refrigerator.
   This butter looks like pink stained glass — beautiful!

Lemon Verbena Jelly

This is such a wonderful jelly to serve with meats. It's also a great spread for toast or biscuits. Make this in late summer for a really special Christmas gift.

    2   cups fresh lemon verbena leaves, cut up
    2 1/2 cups boiling water
    1/4   cup fresh lemon juice
    4 1/2 cups sugar
    1   or 2 drops yellow food coloring
    1   3 ounce package liquid pectin

Place cut up leaves in a large bowl. Pour boiling water over leaves and let stand for 15 minutes. Strain and measure 2 cups of the herb liquid into a heavy saucepan. Add lemon juice and sugar. Stir well and bring to a full rolling boil over high heat, stirring constantly. Add food coloring. Stir in pectin and return to a full rolling boil. Boil hard for 1 minute, stirring constantly. Pour into hot, sterilized jelly jars, leaving 1/4" head space. Adjust lids and process in boiling water bath for 5 minutes. Makes about 2 pints of jelly.

Marie Wallace's World's Best Cookies!

I don't know Marie Wallace, but when she wrote to tell me she liked my book, "It's About Thyme!", she sent this recipe with rave reviews about these cookies. Once in a while a really good and different recipe comes along and this recipe falls into that category. There are interesting additions that you certainly wouldn't expect (corn flakes?!), but the cookie is buttery and very tender — not crisp. They literally melt in your mouth! Thanks, Marie, for one of the best cookie recipes I've tried in a long time.

1	cup butter, softened
1	cup sugar
1	cup light brown sugar, firmly packed
1	egg, slightly beaten
1	cup salad oil (Crisco, Wesson, Puritan, etc.)
1	cup quick rolled oats
1	cup crushed corn flakes (measure after crushing)
3½	cups flour
1	teaspoon baking soda
1	teaspoon salt
1	teaspoon vanilla
½	cup coconut
1	cup pecans, chopped rather fine
	red or green glaceéd cherries for decoration — optional, but pretty on a Holiday cookie tray

Cream butter with the sugars. Add the egg and the oil. Mix well. Add oats, corn flakes, flour, soda, salt and vanilla. Mix well. Stir in coconut and nuts. Roll into 1" balls of dough and place on a lightly greased cookie sheet. Flatten the balls with a fork in a crisscross pattern. Dip fork in water between cookies. If desired, place a glaceéd cherry half in the center of each cookie. Bake at 350° for about 10 minutes, or until light brown. Do not overbake. Makes 8 to 10 dozen cookies.

Cherry Coconut Bars

*The cherries make these bars festive for the Holidays. An easy-to-make gift. Cut these bars into small squares. They are **very** rich!*

2	cups flour
1	cup margarine, melted
6	tablespoons confectioners' sugar
4	eggs, beaten
2	cups sugar
1/2	cup flour
1	teaspoon baking powder
1/2	teaspoon salt
2	teaspoons vanilla
1 1/2	cups chopped nuts
1	cup coconut
1	cup quartered maraschino cherries

Combine the flour, melted margarine and confectioners' sugar. Pat into an ungreased 9" x 13" pan. Bake at 350° for 15 minutes. Beat the eggs, then add remainder of ingredients, except the cherries, to the bowl and mix well. Gently stir cherries into the batter. Spread cherry-nut mixture over the baked crust. Bake about 25 minutes at 350°. Remove from oven. Give the bars a very light dusting of confectioners' sugar. Cool and cut into squares. Makes 2 to 3 dozen bars.

Herb Jelly (A Basic Recipe)

Herb jellies are wonderful accompaniments to meat or seafood dishes. Include a jar or two of these jellies in your gift basket.

2	cups fresh clean herbs*
1	cup boiling water
1	cup cold water
2	cups sugar
	juice of 1 fresh lemon
1	package (or pouch) liquid pectin

Pour the boiling water over the fresh herb leaves and let stand for 15 minutes. Strain into a medium-sized heavy saucepan. Throw away the herbs. Add the cold water, sugar and lemon juice. Bring to a rolling boil. Add the liquid pectin. Stir and bring back to a boil and boil hard for 1 minute. Ladle into sterilized jars. Seal. Makes about 3 cups of jelly.

* Among herbs that make wonderful jelly are thyme, rosemary, lemon verbena, sage, basil, mint or scented geraniums. I usually don't combine herbs for my jellies. I like the singular taste of basil or mint, for example. If desired, put a sprig of fresh, clean herb (used to make the jelly) in each jar before sealing jars.

Cinnamon Honey Butter

*A crock of this delicious butter plus a loaf of homemade bread would make a choice gift.
Each recipe makes 1 cup.*

1	cup butter
1/3	cup honey
1/2	teaspoon ground cinnamon

Place butter in a small mixing bowl and beat on high until butter is light and fluffy. Reduce
speed and gradually drizzle in honey. Add cinnamon and blend thoroughly. Cover and store
for up to 3 weeks in refrigerator. Imagine this butter on homemade biscuits hot from the oven!

Herb Butters

*These herb butter recipes are made with dried herbs. At Christmastime, many of us
don't have the fresh herbs to use. If you are lucky enough to have fresh herbs, just
remember that 1 tablespoon of chopped fresh herbs equals 1 teaspoon of dried herbs, so
adjust the following recipes accordingly.*

Basil Butter

1	cup butter, softened
2	tablespoons dried basil leaves
2	tablespoons dried parsley flakes
2	tablespoons lemon juice
1/2	cup grated Parmesan cheese

Combine butter and seasonings; mix well. Cover and refrigerate for a day to blend flavors. For
gift-giving, pack butter into a small crock or stoneware jar. Keep refrigerated. Add a note
suggesting how to use the butter. (see page 116)

Italian Butter

1	cup butter, softened
1	tablespoon dried oregano
1	teaspoon dried sweet marjoram
1/2	teaspoon garlic powder
1	teaspoon dried parsley flakes
	dash of pepper
1	tablespoon lemon juice

Fines Herbes Butter

1	cup butter, softened
2	tablespoons dried parsley flakes
2	tablespoons freeze-dried chives
1	teaspoon dried French tarragon
1	teaspoon dried chervil leaves
	dash of salt
	dash of pepper

Follow directions for **Basil Butter**.

Top, left to right: Apricot Liqueur, Herbed White Wine Vinegar, Raspberry Vinegar, Orange Wine, Strawberry Vinegar, Christmas Cookies, Popcorn and Nuts. Not pictured: Coffee Liqueur, Steak Marinade, Marinade for Pork Ribs, Seafood Marinade, Yogurt Ginger Marinade, Caramel Apple Dip, Caramel Apples, Hot Fudge Sauce.

Apricot Liqueur

This beautiful and delicious liqueur makes a welcome gift. A sip of this is just right after dessert and coffee. Age the liqueur for two to three weeks before giving or serving.

8	ounces dried apricots, quartered
2	cups water
3/4	cup sugar
2	cups vodka
1	cup brandy
1	2 inch piece cinnamon stick, broken
1/4	teaspoon cardamom seeds

Combine apricots and water in a medium saucepan. Bring to a boil. Reduce heat, cover and simmer for 15 minutes. Cool thoroughly. Combine cooled fruit mixture with the sugar. Stir well. Pour this into a half gallon glass jar. Add vodka, brandy and spices. Stir well. Cover tightly and shake well. Let stand at room temperature for 2 to 3 weeks. Once a day, turn jar over and shake gently to blend flavors and to completely dissolve sugar. When ready to use, strain liqueur through a coffee filter (fitted into a small funnel) into a pretty bottle or decanter. (This will take awhile to drip through.) Cover or cork the container. Makes about 4 cups. I save and serve the apricot pieces with ham or roast pork — very good!

Herbed White Wine Vinegar

All your friends will want a bottle of this vinegar. An easy to make winter vinegar because of the dried herbs used. Each recipe makes two quarts.

2	quarts white wine vinegar
2	tablespoons dried basil
1	tablespoon dried thyme
1	tablespoon dried sweet marjoram
1	tablespoon dried Greek oregano
3	cloves garlic, peeled and chopped
6	whole peppercorns
1/2	teaspoon dried hot pepper flakes
1	tablespoon mustard seeds
1	bay leaf

Put vinegar in a glass or plastic container. Add all herbs and seasonings and stir well. Cover with a nonmetallic lid. Put in a cool, dark place and let steep for 3 weeks to develop flavors. When ready to bottle, fit a coffee filter into a funnel and run the vinegar through filter to make a clear, fragrant and herb-flavored vinegar. Label and cork bottle. This **has** to be good — just look at all the good things in it!

Raspberry Vinegar

I love the fruited vinegars — gorgeous colors and intense flavors. Following is an easy and delicious recipe for raspberry vinegar.

2   10 ounce packages frozen raspberries, thawed and undrained
2   quarts red wine vinegar

Combine raspberries and vinegar in a large glass or plastic container. Cover and let set 48 hours. Transfer mixture to a large saucepan and bring just to a boil. Simmer, uncovered, for 3 minutes. Remove from heat and cool thoroughly. Discard most of the berries, then strain vinegar through a coffee filter into sterilized bottles. Discard the raspberries. Seal or cork and label. Set bottles in a cool, dark place to age for at least 3 weeks before using. Makes 2 quarts.

Use raspberry vinegar to make this simply wonderful vinaigrette: ½ **cup extra virgin olive oil**, ¼ **cup raspberry vinegar** and a **dash of salt**. Dress lettuce or spinach salad with vinaigrette.

Orange Wine

Fruited wines make fabulous gifts. It will take about three weeks to fully develop flavors, so make this orange wine, as well as the cranberry wine, soon after Thanksgiving.

4   medium to large oranges (do not peel)
2   750 ml. bottles of good dry white wine (Chardonnay is a good choice)
1   cup sugar
¼   cup Cognac
     strips of orange zest (no white)

Wash oranges and cut each orange into several pieces. Combine the orange pieces and the wine in a large glass jar. Cover tightly with plastic wrap and secure with a rubber band. Let set in a cool, dark place for 5 days.

   After 5 days, discard orange pieces — I squeeze a handful of these pieces gently as I remove them to add a little juice to the mixture. Strain this orange liquid through a wire strainer (to catch seeds, large pieces of pulp, etc.) into a large bowl. Now add the sugar and Cognac; stir mixture until sugar is completely dissolved. Transfer the wine from the bowl into sterilized bottles through a coffee filter fitted into a small funnel. Insert 1 or 2 long strips of orange peel into each bottle. Cork, label and date. Store bottles in the refrigerator for about 2 weeks before using. Serve the wine chilled. It will keep for several weeks if refrigerated. Makes about 2 quarts of wine.

Strawberry Vinegar

Splash this intensely flavored vinegar on fresh fruits (wonderful on orange slices for a winter salad) or on your next spinach salad. You're in for a pleasant surprise if you haven't tasted this!

2	10 ounce packages frozen strawberries, thawed and undrained
2	quarts white wine vinegar
1/2	cup sugar

Combine strawberries and vinegar in a large glass or plastic container. Cover and let set at room temperature for 48 hours. Stir occasionally. Remove most of strawberry mixture and strain remaining liquid through a coffee filter fitted in a wire strainer. Strain into a large saucepan. Stir in the sugar. Bring just to a boil. Remove from heat and let cool thoroughly. Filter again, if desired, into pretty bottles. Seal or cork, label and enjoy. Makes 2 quarts.

Christmas Cookies

This isn't just another mixed fruit Christmas cookie — it's better than that. The addition of chocolate chips and coconut makes the cookies special. Makes 4 to 5 dozen cookies for gifts. You'll want to save some for yourself.

1/2	cup butter, softened
1	cup sugar
1	large egg, or 2 small eggs, slightly beaten
1	teaspoon vanilla
1 1/4	cups flour
1/2	teaspoon baking soda
1/2	teaspoon salt
1	cup pecans or walnuts, chopped
1	cup semisweet chocolate chips
1	cup grated coconut
1	cup mixed glaceéd fruit, cut up fine

Cream the butter and sugar thoroughly in a large bowl until batter is light and fluffy. Stir in the egg, vanilla, flour, baking soda and salt; mix well. Stir in the nuts, chocolate chips, coconut and fruits; mix to distribute all evenly. The dough is heavy and stiff because of all the fruits and nuts. Drop by heaping teaspoons 2" apart onto greased baking sheets. Bake in a preheated 350° oven for about 15 minutes, or until they're golden. Cool cookies thoroughly. Very, very good.

Popcorn and Nuts

Easy to prepare (candy coating is cooked in microwave oven) and absolutely addictive! I guarantee this will become one of the best gifts you'll make. Makes about 20 cups.

16	cups popped corn (about 3/4 cup popcorn)
1½	cups coarsely chopped pecans*
1½	cups coarsely chopped walnuts*
1	cup light brown sugar, firmly packed
1	stick butter or margarine
½	cup light corn syrup
½	teaspoon salt
½	teaspoon vanilla

Preheat oven to 250°. Pop corn with minimum amount of oil and no salt. Place popped corn and nuts in a large roasting pan. Set pan aside and make the caramel. In a deep 2 quart bowl, combine brown sugar, butter, corn syrup and salt. Place bowl in microwave oven and cook on high for 4 minutes. Rotate bowl a quarter turn and stir or whisk thoroughly. Cook on high for another 3 minutes, or until mixture boils and thickens. Stir in vanilla. Immediately pour hot caramel mixture over the popcorn and nuts. Stir to coat well. Bake mixture, uncovered, in 250° oven for 1 hour, stirring occasionally. Spread mixture onto a large piece of waxed paper to cool. Stir to separate big chunks. As soon as it's cool, store in airtight containers. When not munching on it, be sure to keep contents in tightly covered containers.

* You can substitute 3 cups roasted, salted peanuts for the pecans and walnuts.

Coffee Liqueur

No gift could be easier to make than this one. If you like the high-priced Mexican version, you'll really like this — it's relatively inexpensive to make and truly does taste almost like the real thing! Makes about 2 quarts.

3	cups sugar
1	cup instant coffee dry granules
4	cups water
1	quart vodka
3	teaspoons vanilla extract

Combine sugar, coffee and water in a large saucepan. Stir and bring mixture to a boil. Reduce heat and simmer for 1 hour (simmer, not boil). Remove from heat and cool to room temperature. Add vodka and vanilla. Place mixture in a large glass jar. Cover tightly and age in a cool, dark place for about 4 weeks. When ready to use, strain liqueur through a coffee filter that's fitted into a small funnel. This may take awhile because liqueur is somewhat thickened by now. If you're presenting this liqueur as a gift, be sure to say that besides using this liqueur as an after-dinner drink, it's also delicious poured over ice cream or other desserts.

Marvelous Marinades

*M*arinades **are** marvelous because of what they do for meats and other foods. Typically, a marinade has three parts to it: 1) an **acid** that breaks down muscle fiber, 2) an **oil** that coats and seals the outside of the meat, and 3) **aromatics**, such as herbs, spices, aromatic seeds, etc. These so-called aromatics add the flavor.

As you think about marinades, you'll remember that there is usually a fruit juice or vinegar or soy sauce added. These act as the **acid** part of the marinade. You'll see that one of my marinades has yogurt in it. Since yogurt is a type of soured milk, it too acts as an acid. Yogurt is widely used in the Middle East and South America in marinades.

Many **oils** can be used in your marinades. I like olive oil, especially extra virgin, because of its wonderful flavor, but I also use sesame oil, corn or soybean oil and even walnut and hazelnut oil in marinades.

As for herbs and spices and other **aromatics** to use, some of the obvious ones are garlic, onions, ground ginger or fresh gingerroot, cinnamon stick pieces, bay leaves or whole peppercorns. A little sugar or honey is often added to provide a crusty surface. In the summer, or growing season, add fresh aromatic herbs (in place of dried ones), such as rosemary, thyme, oregano, etc. To release the flavor of these fresh herbs, slightly bruise the leaves before adding them to the marinade ingredients. Remember that it takes about three times as much fresh herb as dried herb to deliver the same flavor. Also remember, you may use one of these aromatics, or a combination of them.

I find that for seafood or fish, a perfect marinade is made with fresh lemon or lime juice, olive oil and herbs such as basil, Greek oregano, sweet marjoram, dill, chives, French tarragon and thyme (use one or a combination of herbs). A basic recipe for a simple fish marinade is: **1 cup extra virgin olive oil, juice of 1 lemon,** and **1 or 2 tablespoons chopped fresh herb** (any of those listed above), or 1 or 2 teaspoons dried herb, if fresh isn't available. You may add **salt, chopped garlic, chopped green onions**, etc., to add more flavor. Fish or seafood needs only to marinate an hour or so, the first half hour in the refrigerator and the last half hour at room temperature. Now you're ready to bake, fry, broil or grill the fish.

A good basic chicken marinade is: **1 cup vegetable oil, 4 to 6 tablespoons herb vinegar, fruit-flavored vinegar** (such as raspberry), or just plain **cider vinegar**, and **2 to 3 tablespoons chopped fresh herb**, such as basil, rosemary, oregano, sweet marjoram, chives, sage, French tarragon, or thyme, or 2 to 3 teaspoons dried herb. And of course, you may want to add from the aromatic category, such as garlic, onion, gingerroot, etc. I like to marinate chicken pieces 2 to 4 hours. Marinate chicken in refrigerator except the last hour when you bring chicken and marinade to room temperature. Chicken is ready to cook as desired.

A basic marinade for red meats is: **1 cup vegetable or olive oil, 1 cup red wine vinegar**, and **2 to 3 tablespoons chopped fresh herbs**, such as rosemary, oregano, sweet marjoram, summer savory, sage and thyme, or 2 to 3 teaspoons dried herbs. Add soy sauce, garlic, onions, salt and pepper, peppercorns, bay leaf and even flakes of dried hot chili pepper to spice up the marinade. The red meats usually require several hours or overnight of marinating in order to tenderize and flavor properly.

When you're ready to cook anything that's been marinating, be sure to blot the meat thoroughly to remove most of the marinade from the surface of the meat. I use several layers of paper toweling. If you don't remove the marinade, the meat will blacken and burn as it cooks.

The three basic recipes above (seafood, poultry, red meat) will make enough to marinate about 3 pounds of meat. You can reduce or enlarge these recipes to suit your needs. Some recipes say to reuse marinades, but I think it's safer to use only once, then throw it away.

Use your imagination when making marinades! Follow a basic recipe and add what you like for the special flavors.

Besides the above basic recipes for marinades, the following four recipes are marvelous indeed!

Steak Marinade

This recipe makes about 3 cups of marinade, so it's perfect to divide for gifts and even keep some for yourself.

- 2   cups vegetable oil
- 1   tablespoon Kitchen Bouquet (browning and seasoning sauce)
- 3/4   cup soy sauce
- 1   teaspoon Worcestershire sauce
- 1   teaspoon paprika
- 2   teaspoons salt
- 1/2   teaspoon garlic powder
- 1/2   teaspoon onion salt
- 1/2   teaspoon black pepper

Combine all ingredients and mix well. Store in an airtight container in the refrigerator. To use, marinate steaks or chops in this marinade for 4 hours or more. Blot excess marinade off meat and broil or grill. Baste lightly with the marinade as you cook.

Marinade for Pork Ribs

If you're tired of the usual barbecued ribs, try marinating them the next time. Better double the recipe and keep some for yourself. Basic recipe is enough marinade for about 3 pounds of ribs.

- 1/2   cup dry sherry
- 1/2   cup teriyaki sauce
- 1/4   cup fresh orange juice
- 2   teaspoons sesame oil
- 2   tablespoons fresh gingerroot, peeled and minced
- 2   tablespoons fresh parsley or cilantro, chopped
- 1   tablespoon garlic, minced
- 1   tablespoon orange rind, grated fine (use only orange part — no white)
- 1/4   teaspoon pepper

Combine all ingredients. Put about 3 pounds of ribs in a large, shallow baking dish (not metal). Pour marinade over ribs, cover and marinate for 6 hours, or even overnight, in the refrigerator. Turn occasionally. About 1 hour before cooking ribs, remove them from the refrigerator and let them come to room temperature. Now put the dish containing the ribs and marinade in a 350° oven for 45 minutes (your kitchen will smell terrific!). Remove pan from the oven. Lift ribs from marinade. Blot with paper towels and place on preheated charcoal grill. Grill for about 20 to 30 minutes, turning and basting ribs several times with the marinade. Serves 4 to 6 — 4 is more realistic, though!

Seafood Marinade

Make this marvelous marinade in the summer when you have fresh basil. It can be made and frozen for later use, if desired. I treat this marinade just like I treat pesto that I'm freezing. After the marinade is in the freezer container, pour a thin layer of olive oil over the top to keep the marinade (or pesto) from discoloring.

2	cloves garlic
2	tablespoons fresh basil
2	teaspoons Dijon mustard
2	tablespoons fresh lemon juice
2	tablespoons white wine vinegar
3/4	cup extra virgin olive oil
	salt and pepper

Mince garlic and basil in food processor. Add remaining ingredients and process until mixture is smooth. Cover and marinate fish or seafood for about 30 minutes in the refrigerator. Remove from refrigerator 30 minutes before using. Blot excess marinade, then broil or grill.

Yogurt Ginger Marinade

I ordered chicken breast marinated in a ginger-yogurt sauce in a wonderful Lebanese restaurant in London. They didn't choose to divulge their marinade recipe, but this one is pretty close to that taste. Tell the person receiving this gift to keep it refrigerated!

2	teaspoons fresh gingerroot, minced
3	cloves garlic, minced
2	cups low fat plain yogurt
1/4	cup fresh lemon juice
2	bay leaves, crumbled
2	tablespoons paprika
1	teaspoon ground coriander seeds
1	teaspoon ground cumin seeds
1	teaspoon ground cinnamon
1	teaspoon turmeric
1/2	teaspoon ground pepper
1/4	teaspoon ground cardamom seeds
1	teaspoon salt, or more to taste

Peel gingerroot and mince it fine. Do the same with the garlic. Combine all ingredients in a medium bowl — use a wire whisk and blend thoroughly. Marinate chicken breast halves in this marinade, covered, for about 2 hours in the refrigerator. Remove chicken from the refrigerator about 30 minutes before cooking. Remove pieces from marinade, blot off excess and grill or broil.

Caramel Apple Dip

Another great recipe from my friend, Annie. Serve this dip with unpeeled apple wedges, or spoon a little of the warmed sauce over baked apples, or use as an ice cream or cake topping — there are so many ways to use this delicious dip. Not only is it good, it's so easy to put together in your microwave.

1	stick butter
1	cup light or dark brown sugar, firmly packed
1/2	cup light or dark corn syrup
1	can condensed milk (not evaporated)

Melt butter in the microwave oven. Add brown sugar, corn syrup and condensed milk and whisk all together. Cook uncovered in microwave on high for 2 minutes. Remove from oven and whisk vigorously. Cook another minute in the microwave. Remove from oven and whisk again. Cool, cover and refrigerate.

To use, heat the dip in the microwave for a few seconds and whisk or stir until smooth. Dip apple wedges in the warm sauce.

Caramel Apples

Old fashioned caramel apples are a treat for young and old alike. Any child or teenager on your list would like a gift of these. Be sure to use firm, best quality apples with no blemishes or soft spots. I like crisp Red Delicious.

2	sticks butter (no substitute)
2	cups light brown sugar, firmly packed
1	cup light corn syrup
1	15 ounce can sweetened condensed milk
1	teaspoon vanilla
	chopped pecans, if desired
8	wooden sticks
8	medium to large Red Delicious apples

This recipe requires a 3 quart heavy saucepan and a reliable candy thermometer. Melt butter in the saucepan. Stir in sugar, corn syrup and condensed milk. Mix well. Bring to a boil over medium heat, stirring occasionally. Cook to firm ball stage (245°), stirring frequently. This will take longer than you think — at least 15 minutes, or more. Remove pan from heat and stir in vanilla. Have waxed paper cut and spread out. If using nuts, spread nuts on waxed paper. Put a wooden stick in each apple core. Dip apple into the hot caramel mixture almost to top of apple. Set apple down on the chopped pecans and press slightly to imbed the nuts into the caramel. Allow caramel to set. Store in a cool, dry place, but do not refrigerate. Best if used within 2 or 3 days.

For a gift, set each apple in a square of plastic wrap. Draw wrap up around apple and tie with a pretty ribbon. Recipe makes enough caramel to cover 8 or perhaps 9 apples. If you very lightly grease the plastic wrap, the wrap won't stick to the apple.

Hot Fudge Sauce

Add a jar of this delicious sauce to a gift basket for some lucky friend. Keep the sauce refrigerated.

1	cup unsweetened cocoa
1½	cups sugar
1	cup light brown sugar, firmly packed
¼	teaspoon salt
2	cups heavy cream
2	sticks butter, cut into pieces
2	teaspoons vanilla

In a heavy saucepan, combine cocoa, the sugars and salt. Add cream and butter and cook over medium heat, stirring constantly. Bring to a boil. Boil 1 minute, stirring constantly. Remove from heat. Cover and cool for 5 minutes. Stir in vanilla. Makes 4 to 5 cups of rich chocolate sauce.

Variation: For a lighter, creamier sauce, add **1 jar (7 ounce size) of marshmallow creme** after you stir in the vanilla. Stir until the creme is melted and sauce is smooth.

Top, left to right: Old Fashioned Applesauce Cake with Caramel Glaze, Pumpkin Cookies with Ginger Cream Cheese Frosting, Minted Coffee Mix in Santa Mug, Peanut Cookies, Whole Wheat Honey Potato Bread, Honey and Herb Bread. Not pictured: Sue Riggs' Special Pumpkin Muffins, Brown Sugar Meringue-Topped Peanut Bars, Cranberry Sauce Cake, Mae's Peanut Butter Goodies, Peanut Butter Cake with Chocolate Peanut Butter Frosting.

Old Fashioned Applesauce Cake
with Caramel Glaze

*Do you have special memories of a cake your grandmother made for the Holidays?
This could very well be the cake in your memory! It is dark, rich and very spicy. The
caramel glaze is the best I've ever tasted!*

1	cup butter
2	cups sugar
2	eggs
3	cups sifted flour
1½	teaspoons ground nutmeg
1	teaspoon ground cloves
1	tablespoon ground cinnamon
1	tablespoon baking soda
½	teaspoon salt
2½	cups thick applesauce (a 24 ounce jar)
1	tablespoon light corn syrup
1	cup light raisins
1	cup chopped walnuts, black walnuts or pecans
	Barbara Glover's Caramel Glaze (recipe on next page)

Cream butter and sugar. Gradually beat in eggs, one at a time. Sift together the flour, nutmeg, cloves, cinnamon, baking soda and salt. Remove ¼ cup and set aside. In a small bowl, mix applesauce and corn syrup thoroughly. Add applesauce mixture alternately with flour mixture to the creamed mixture. In another small bowl, mix the reserved ¼ cup dry ingredients into the raisins and nuts. Add this to batter and gently stir all together. Pour batter into a greased and floured tube pan. Bake at 300° for 1½ hours. Check after 1¼ hours, and if browning too much, lay a piece of foil on top. Cake may take a little longer to bake — a tester must come out clean. To complete the cake, follow Barbara Glover's Caramel Glaze recipe on the next page. Cake will serve 12 to 16.

Barbara Glover's Caramel Glaze

*Barbara brought an apple cake with this glaze on it to a carry-in supper. I was lucky enough to be there and Barbara was nice enough to share the recipe. This glaze won't turn to sugar (as many caramel glazes do) and it's superb on apple cake, applesauce cake, or most **any** cake!*

1	cup light brown sugar, firmly packed
1	cup granulated sugar
4	tablespoons flour
1½	cups cold water
1	stick margarine
1	teaspoon vanilla
	whole walnut or pecan halves, for decoration

A few minutes before the cake is done, combine the brown sugar, granulated sugar, flour, cold water and margarine in a medium saucepan. Cook until sauce is clear and thick, about 15 to 20 minutes, stirring occasionally with a wire whisk. Add the vanilla. Remove pan from the stove.

   When cake comes out of the oven, cool cake long enough to be able to remove it from the pan. Place cake on serving plate. Stir the warm glaze and pour it over the warm cake. Decorate top with walnut or pecan halves, if desired.

   Cool cake completely. Wrap cake for freezer, if desired, and store for up to 1 month. For a special gift, you may wish to present the wrapped cake on a pretty cake plate, and perhaps even attach the recipe!

Pumpkin Cookies with Ginger Cream Cheese Frosting

This is an extraordinarily good cookie. They are very good plain, but spread on a little Ginger Cream Cheese Frosting and they are superb! These cookies, along with the recipe, make a wonderful gift. Makes about 4 dozen cookies.

2½	cups flour
½	teaspoon baking soda
¼	teaspoon salt
2	teaspoons pumpkin pie spice (Spice Islands is truly the best)
1	cup dark brown sugar, firmly packed
½	cup granulated sugar
¾	cup butter, softened
1	large egg
1	cup canned pumpkin
1	teaspoon vanilla
1	cup raisins
1	cup walnuts, chopped

In a medium bowl, combine the first 4 ingredients. Set bowl aside. In mixer bowl, combine and mix the sugars, then add the butter and beat well. Scrape down sides of bowl and mix again. Now add the egg, pumpkin and vanilla. Mix until light and fluffy. At low speed, blend in the flour mixture. Add the raisins and nuts and mix only until blended. Drop by tablespoonfuls onto ungreased cookie sheets, about 2" apart. Bake at 350° for 20 to 24 minutes, or until cookies test done when touched in the middle. Cool cookies and frost with the following.

Ginger Cream Cheese Frosting

3	ounces cream cheese, at room temperature
4	tablespoons butter, at room temperature
⅛	teaspoon ground ginger
2	to 2½ cups confectioners' sugar, sifted
2	tablespoons (or more) water

Beat the cream cheese, butter and ground ginger together until light and fluffy. Add the confectioners' sugar and thin with water to proper spreading consistency. Spread a thin layer of frosting on each cookie.

Minted Coffee Mix

This is a perfect last-minute gift for the teacher or anyone else you need a little gift for. It's especially nice to give along with a coffee cup or mug. Each recipe makes about 12 servings.

$1/3$	cup sugar
$1/4$	cup powdered coffee creamer
$1/4$	cup instant coffee
2	peppermint hard candies, finely crushed (I like the red pinwheel peppermint candies)

Put candies in a plastic bag and crush them with a hammer or rolling pin. Now combine all ingredients and store in an airtight container. Add a note saying: "For each serving, stir 1 tablespoon of coffee mix into 6 ounces of boiling water. Stir to melt all ingredients."

Peanut Cookies

Peanuts are a wonderful addition to cookies! When I was much younger, I remember having peanut cookies at a church supper. Someone gave this recipe to me not long ago. I tried it and I believe it is very close to that cookie. At any rate, a plate of these would make a great gift.

$1^3/4$	cups salted, roasted peanuts, divided (not dry roasted)
$1^1/2$	cups flour
$1/2$	teaspoon baking soda
$1/2$	cup butter or margarine, softened
$3/4$	cup light brown sugar, firmly packed
$3/4$	cup granulated sugar
1	large egg, or 2 small eggs
1	tablespoon water
$1/2$	teaspoon vanilla

Finely chop $1^1/2$ cups of peanuts in food processor. Combine flour and soda in a small bowl. In another bowl, beat butter and both sugars until light. To this mixture, add the chopped peanuts, egg, water and vanilla. Mix until smooth. Stir in the flour mixture.

Lightly flour a work surface and scrape dough onto that surface. Roll dough into 1" balls (no larger!) and place on a greased cookie sheet. Flour the bottom of a glass and flatten each ball to about $3/8$" thick. Coarsely chop the remaining $1/4$ cup of peanuts and press some nuts onto each cookie. Bake in a 375° oven about 10 minutes, or until golden brown. Do not overbake. Cool cookies and wrap well to freeze or store in airtight containers. Makes about 6 dozen cookies. These are delicious cookies.

Whole Wheat Honey Potato Bread

Mother always said the addition of potatoes, or potato water, to a yeast bread recipe made the bread more flavorful and also it would have wonderful texture. I certainly find that to be true with this old favorite recipe.

1½	cups water
1¼	cups milk
¼	cup butter or margarine
¼	cup honey
3½	cups bread flour, or unbleached flour
2½	to 3 cups whole wheat flour
1½	cups instant mashed potato flakes
2½	teaspoons salt
2	packages active dry yeast
2	eggs

In a large saucepan, heat the first 4 ingredients until very warm (120°). Don't guess. Use a candy thermometer. Combine the flours in a large bowl and set aside. In a large mixer bowl, combine the warm liquid, 2 cups of the mixed flour, potato flakes, salt, yeast and eggs. Beat 4 minutes at medium speed. Stir in, by hand, as much flour as you can. When you can no longer incorporate the flour, dump the remainder of the flour onto your kneading surface (this could be as much as 2 cups or more of flour). Knead dough until smooth and elastic, about 5 minutes, pulling in flour as you need it to make a smooth and elastic ball. Don't worry if there is ½ cup or so flour left on your surface. Place ball in a greased bowl. Cover with a clean cloth and let rise until doubled, about 1 hour.

Generously grease 2 loaf pans (9" x 5"). Punch down dough and divide and shape into 2 loaves. Place in prepared pans. Cover and let rise until doubled, 30 to 45 minutes. Bake in a preheated 375°* oven for 35 to 40 minutes until a deep golden brown. If loaves are browning too much, loosely cover with foil the last 10 to 15 minutes of baking time. Remove from the oven and let pans cool about 5 minutes. Remove loaves from pans and brush tops with a little melted butter for a soft crust. Makes 2 great loaves for gifts (or even for yourself!).

* Reduce heat to 350° if using glass baking pans.

Honey and Herb Bread

This recipe makes three beautiful loaves of bread. Give the recipe and some suggested uses — especially good in a chicken salad or tuna salad sandwich and wonderful toasted for breakfast with honey butter.

2	packages active dry yeast
$^1/_2$	cup warm water (105° to 115°)
1	tablespoon honey
3	cups milk
$^1/_4$	cup plus 1 tablespoon olive oil
$^1/_4$	cup honey
2	tablespoons butter or margarine
1	teaspoon dried parsley
1	teaspoon dried basil
1	teaspoon dried oregano
1	teaspoon dried celery flakes
1	teaspoon dried onion flakes
$^1/_4$	teaspoon dried thyme
8	to 8$^1/_2$ cups bread flour
1	cup whole wheat flour
1$^1/_2$	teaspoons salt

Dissolve yeast in warm water. Stir in the 1 tablespoon honey. Set aside. Combine milk, olive oil, the $^1/_4$ cup of honey, butter and the seasonings in a large, heavy saucepan. Heat to 105°. Stir in the yeast mixture. Combine flour and salt in a large mixing bowl. Add milk mixture. Stir until all dry ingredients are moistened. Turn dough out onto a heavily floured work surface and knead for 5 minutes. Dough must be smooth and elastic. Put dough in a well-greased bowl. Grease all sides of dough. Cover bowl with a clean cloth and let rise in a warm place for about 1 hour, or until doubled. Punch down dough.

Turn onto a floured surface and cover with the cloth. Let dough rest for 5 minutes. Knead dough 3 or 4 times and divide it into thirds. Place each third into a well-greased 9" x 5" loaf pan. Again, cover the pans with a clean cloth and let rise for 30 to 45 minutes, or until dough comes just above rim of pan. Bake at 350° for 45 minutes or until loaves sound hollow when tapped. After 30 minutes of baking, if loaves appear to be browning too much, lay a piece of foil over each pan, then continue baking. Let cool a few minutes, then turn loaves out to cool completely. Wrap well and freeze, if desired, for up to 1 month.

Sue Riggs' Special Pumpkin Muffins

Sue has greatly reduced the fat in these muffins and also reduced the cholesterol. I'm sure there is someone on your list who would appreciate a plateful of these.

1	cup whole wheat flour
1/2	cup unbleached white flour
1/2	cup regular rolled oats
2	teaspoons baking powder
1	teaspoon ground cinnamon
1/2	teaspoon salt
1/2	teaspoon ground ginger
1/2	teaspoon ground mace
1/8	teaspoon ground cloves
1/4	teaspoon baking soda
2	egg whites, slightly beaten
1	cup canned pumpkin
1/2	cup light molasses
1/2	cup orange juice
1/4	cup cooking oil
1/2	cup chopped walnuts or pecans

Combine and blend the first 10 ingredients. Add egg whites, pumpkin, molasses, orange juice, oil and nuts. Mix well. Spray muffin pans with nonstick vegetable spray. Bake at 375° for 20 to 25 minutes. Makes 12 muffins. Each muffin is about 200 calories.

Brown Sugar Meringue-Topped Peanut Bars

You'll make a real hit with someone when you give them a plateful of these! This recipe comes from a friend in Minnesota.

2	cups flour
2	teaspoons baking powder
1	teaspoon baking soda
1/2	teaspoon salt
1/2	cup shortening
1/2	cup sugar
1/2	cup light brown sugar, firmly packed
2	egg yolks (save whites)
1	teaspoon vanilla
3	tablespoons cold water
1	12 ounce package semisweet chocolate chips
2	egg whites
1	cup light brown sugar, firmly packed
1	cup salted peanuts

Sift together the flour, baking powder, baking soda and salt. Set aside. In a large mixer bowl, cream shortening and sugars until well mixed. Stir in egg yolks and vanilla. Add cold water alternately with the sifted dry ingredients to make a stiff dough. Grease and flour a 15" x 10" x 1" jelly roll pan. Pat dough into the pan. Sprinkle chocolate chips evenly over the dough. Beat egg whites until foamy. Gradually add brown sugar and beat until whites are stiff. Spread mixture over the chocolate chips. Sprinkle peanuts evenly over the top. Bake at 325° for 30 to 35 minutes. Cut into bars while still warm. Yields 3 to 4 dozen bars, depending on how you cut them.

Cranberry Sauce Cake

This cake is so easy (mixes in one bowl) and very rich and moist. Make one for yourself and make another one for a special friend.

1	16 ounce can whole berry cranberry sauce
1	cup mayonnaise (the real thing)
1	tablespoon grated orange rind
1/3	cup orange juice
1	cup chopped walnuts
3	cups flour
1 1/2	cups sugar
1	teaspoon baking soda
1	teaspoon salt
1	teaspoon orange extract

Cut brown paper (I use a grocery bag) to fit the bottom of a tube pan. Spray the pan and the paper with a nonstick vegetable spray. Combine all cake ingredients in a large bowl and mix well. Pour batter into prepared pan and bake at 350° for 1 to 1 1/4 hours, or until cake tests done. Cool cake long enough to be able to remove it from the pan. Serve cake plain, or drizzle a little confectioners' sugar icing on top and down sides. For the icing, I use **1 cup sifted confectioners' sugar** thinned with **orange juice** to make a thin glaze. Put glaze on warm cake. Cool cake completely. Cake may be wrapped well and frozen for up to 1 month.

Mae's Peanut Butter Goodies

Once a year (each November), the women in my church gather for our annual project of baking fruitcakes to sell. We wear ourselves out, but we must love it, because come next November, we're at it again! Sometimes, one of us will make or bake something and bring it in to share at lunchtime. We all fell for these cookies of Mae's because they could be put together so quickly, and they didn't require baking. Every one of us wrote down and took home this recipe!

2	sticks butter or margarine, melted
1/3	cup crushed graham crackers
1	cup chunky peanut butter
1	1 pound box confectioners' sugar, sifted
1	12 ounce package milk chocolate chips

Combine melted butter, graham cracker crumbs, peanut butter and confectioners' sugar. Mix well and press into the bottom of a 9" x 13" pan. Melt the chocolate chips and quickly spread them over the cookie mixture. Cut into serving pieces before chocolate gets too hard. This recipe makes 3 or 4 dozen cookies, depending on how large you cut them.

Put these in a pretty Christmas tin (with waxed paper between the layers) for some lucky person on your list.

Peanut Butter Cake with Chocolate Peanut Butter Frosting

This is a wonderful cake for any time of the year. Give one to a friend in a nice new 9-inch cake pan. Each time she uses that pan, she'll think about you and the special cake that came in it!

1/2	cup shortening (I use 1 stick margarine)
1/2	cup chunky peanut butter
1 1/2	cups light brown sugar, firmly packed
1	teaspoon vanilla
2/3	cup milk
1 1/2	cups sifted cake flour
2	teaspoons baking powder
	Chocolate Peanut Butter Frosting (recipe follows)

Beat shortening, peanut butter, brown sugar, vanilla and milk with an electric mixer until light and fluffy. Combine flour and baking powder and mix into the batter. Place into a greased and floured 9" square baking pan. Bake in a 350° oven for 40 to 50 minutes, or until cake tests done. If cake is not done after 40 minutes, lay a piece of foil over the cake and continue to bake until the cake is done. Cool cake, then frost. Cake serves 9. I should tell you — this cake usually falls in the middle! But that's okay — just fill with icing and everyone will be happy!

Chocolate Peanut Butter Frosting

1 1/2	cups sifted confectioners' sugar
4	tablespoons cocoa powder
1/4	cup butter or margarine, softened
1/3	cup chunky peanut butter
	milk to moisten

Combine confectioners' sugar, cocoa, butter and peanut butter. Add milk to make frosting spreadable.

Top, left to right: Fruit 'n Fiber Bread, Cupcake Brownies, Mother's Coconut Apricot Pineapple Squares, Glazed Pecans, Mint Tea. Not pictured: Maple Nut Fudge, Peanut Butter Fudge, Pumpkin Walnut Fudge, Herbed Olive Oil, Ornaments to Paint, 11 Spice Chicken Seasonings, Great Granola, 7 Beans and 1 Great Soup.

Fruit 'n Fiber Bread

Two delicious loaves equal two delicious gifts! Or keep one loaf for Christmas breakfast. This is a dark, dense bread.

2	cups boiling water
1¹/₂	cups chopped prunes
¹/₂	cup raisins
3	eggs
³/₄	cup light brown sugar, firmly packed
2	cups whole wheat flour
2	teaspoons baking powder
1	teaspoon baking soda
1	teaspoon ground cinnamon
¹/₂	teaspoon ground cloves
2	cups bran
1	cup chopped nuts

Preheat oven to 350°. Pour boiling water over the prunes and raisins. Set aside. In a large bowl, beat eggs until light. Continue beating while adding brown sugar. When light and creamy, add 1 cup of the wheat flour (sift this 1 cup with the baking powder, baking soda, cinnamon and cloves). Now stir in half of the prune mixture and then the rest of the wheat flour and the bran. Stir in remainder of the prune mixture and the nuts. Pour into 2 greased and lightly floured 9" x 5" loaf pans. Bake for about 45 to 55 minutes or until done. If using glass pans, reduce heat to 325°.

Cupcake Brownies

You'll use this recipe over and over again. You can successfully double this recipe and make enough for friends, as well as yourself! Anyone on your list would love these.

2	sticks margarine
4	ounces semisweet chocolate
4	eggs
1³/₄	cups sugar
1	cup flour
1	cup chopped walnuts or pecans

Melt margarine and chocolate together in a fairly large pan. Remove pan from stove and let mixture cool a few minutes. Add remainder of ingredients and mix, but do not overmix. Spoon batter into foil-lined cupcake pans (use either regular-sized pans or the mini cupcake pans — just be sure to use the foil cupcake pan liners). Fill cups ¹/₂ full. Bake at 325° for about 30 minutes (adjust time if using mini pans). Let cool. If desired, spread a little of your favorite chocolate confectioners' sugar frosting on each cupcake. May be wrapped well and frozen. Makes about 2 dozen regular size brownies, or 3¹/₂ to 4 dozen mini brownies. On a scale of 1 to 10, these are definitely a 10!

Mother's Coconut Apricot Pineapple Squares

I recently found this recipe of Mother's as I was going through her old collection. I had forgotten about these cookies, but as soon as I read it, it brought back fond memories of sweet-tart cookies that she used to make. A box or plateful of these would surely be a welcome gift.

- $1/2$ cup shortening
- 2 egg yolks (save whites)
- $1/2$ cup confectioners' sugar
- 1 cup flour
- $1/2$ cup apricot preserves
- $1/2$ cup pineapple preserves
- 2 egg whites
- $1/2$ cup granulated sugar
- $1/2$ cup coconut

Cream thoroughly the shortening, egg yolks and confectioners' sugar. Add the 1 cup flour and mix well. Pat into a greased 8" x 8" baking pan. Bake at 350° for about 15 minutes, or until crust is golden brown. As soon as the crust comes out of the oven, mix the 2 preserves together and spread on the warm crust. Now beat the egg whites together with the granulated sugar until stiff peaks form. Fold in the coconut. Spread meringue mixture on the crust and bake at 350° for about 30 minutes. Cool and cut into small squares. An absolutely wonderful cookie! Makes about 3 dozen squares.

Glazed Pecans

There isn't a nicer gift than one of pecans. This is a terrific way to prepare pecans for gift-giving. Give them in glass jars with bows on top.

- $1/4$ cup unsalted butter
- $1/4$ cup light corn syrup
- 2 tablespoons water
- 1 teaspoon salt
- 1 pound pecan halves

Preheat oven to 250°. Line a baking sheet with foil. Combine butter, corn syrup, water and salt in a heavy, small saucepan. Bring to a boil. Stir in pecans and mix well to coat pecans on all sides. Spread evenly on baking sheet and bake for 40 minutes, stirring every 10 minutes. Makes 4 cups.

Herbal Teas

An herbal tea is simply fresh or dried leaves of certain herbs which are then steeped in boiling water to draw out the herb flavor. Choose one herb or a combination of herbs, experiment a little and you'll learn to enjoy these wonderfully soothing and fragrant teas. Many of these teas are considered to have medicinal qualities. My basic method for making an herbal tea is . . .

With fresh herb leaves

Put **1 tablespoon fresh herb leaves** in the bottom of your tea pot; add **2 cups boiling water**. Let steep for 3 to 5 minutes. Pour tea through a strainer into tea cup. Makes 2 cups of tea. If you like stronger tea, add more herb leaves — if you like weaker tea, add less.

With dried herbs

Put **1 teaspoon dried herb leaves** in the bottom of your tea pot and proceed with directions above.

Some wonderful herbs to use, fresh or dried, for your teas are the following:

Lemon verbena — my favorite. Add a teaspoon or so of honey per cup, if desired, or sugar to taste if you want a sweet tea.

Mint* — there are so many great mints. I love ginger mint, lavender mint, candy mint, orange mint or old fashioned spearmint or peppermint for tea. Actually, any culinary mint makes a great cup of tea!

Chamomile — this herb makes a pale colored tea that tastes faintly of apples.

Basil — a spicy, clove-like flavor. Add a couple of whole cloves to reinforce the clove taste.

Clover — clover makes a good cup of tea. It is also readily available. Clover tea has a delicate, sweet taste. I usually air-dry the blossoms a few days, then use 2 heaping teaspoons of the dried blossoms for 2 cups of boiling water. Sweeten with clover honey.

Scented geraniums — you can take your pick of dozens of varieties of the scented geraniums. I particularly like apricot, lemon, nutmeg, rose, rose geranium, apple and coconut. I think fresh scented geranium leaves are best for this tea. The dried leaves often lose much of their fragrance and flavor. For 2 cups of tea, cut and slightly crush 1 large leaf, or several small ones (such as the small nutmeg leaves).

For a beautiful gift, perhaps you could find an antique tea caddy or tin or an antique cup and saucer and give this filled with dried herb leaves along with the recipe for making the tea. Be sure to seal the tea leaves in a plastic bag, plastic wrap, or cellophane. This will keep the leaves fresh and fragrant.

* *While you have plenty of fresh mint in the garden, be sure to make some mint ice cubes. Combine 4 cups water and 1 cup sugar in a small saucepan. Boil for 5 minutes. Cover pan and cool. Clean 20 to 30 fresh mint leaves. Bruise each leaf slightly to release the oil and place one leaf in each compartment of ice cube trays. Pour sugar-water mixture over each leaf. Freeze. When cubes are frozen, pop each cube out and place cubes in a zip-lock bag. Immediately put back in freezer.*
Flavor teas or other drinks with these cubes. A nice taste of summer any time of the year.

Maple Nut Fudge

An easy-to-make chocolate fudge, but with maple flavoring added. The one on your list who receives a box of this fudge will be lucky indeed.

4	tablespoons butter
4½	cups sugar
¼	teaspoon salt
1	11 to 12 ounce can evaporated milk
1	12 ounce package semisweet chocolate chips
8	ounces bittersweet chocolate, broken into small pieces
1	7 ounce jar marshmallow creme
1	teaspoon maple flavoring
2	cups chopped walnuts

Combine butter, sugar, salt and evaporated milk in a heavy medium saucepan. Bring to a boil and boil for 7 minutes. Combine the chocolates, the marshmallow creme, flavoring and nuts in a large glass bowl. Slowly add milk mixture and stir with a wooden spoon until well mixed. You must stir vigorously until the candy is stiff — may take several minutes. Pour candy into a well-buttered 9" x 13" pan. Cover with plastic wrap or foil and refrigerate for several hours. Cut into desired size pieces. Makes about 2 to 2½ pounds.

Peanut Butter Fudge

I have made this several times for gifts and it's no-fail. I usually wrap individual pieces in plastic wrap and pack them into a Christmas box or tin. If you're giving the candy to someone who likes to cook, be sure to give them the recipe also.

1	16 ounce package light brown sugar
1	5 ounce can evaporated milk
4	tablespoons butter
1	teaspoon cider vinegar
1	teaspoon vanilla
1	12 ounce jar chunky peanut butter

Mix together the brown sugar, evaporated milk, butter and vinegar in a heavy 2½ to 3 quart saucepan. Cook over medium-low heat to boiling, stirring constantly. Put candy thermometer in pan and continue to cook (but don't stir) until temperature reaches 238°. Remove saucepan from heat. Use a wooden spoon and beat candy until it begins to thicken. Stir in vanilla and peanut butter; blend well. Pour into a greased 8" square pan. Cool, then cover pan and refrigerate candy until firm. When cold, cut into desired size pieces. Makes about 2 pounds of delicious candy.

Pumpkin Walnut Fudge

*I just recently tried pumpkin fudge for the first time. I had no idea it was so good!
A delicious gift.*

4	cups sugar
1	cup whole milk
1	cup canned pumpkin
1/4	teaspoon ground nutmeg
1/4	teaspoon ground cinnamon
3	tablespoons dark corn syrup
	pinch of salt
3	tablespoons unsalted butter, cut into pieces
2	cups chopped toasted walnuts*
1	teaspoon vanilla

Combine sugar, milk, pumpkin, spices, corn syrup and salt in a large, heavy saucepan over
medium-high heat. Heat to a boil, then cook until a candy thermometer reads 238°. Do not stir
during this time. Remove pan from the stove and add the pieces of butter. Do not stir it into
the mixture. Leave thermometer in pan and let candy stand until thermometer reads 140°. Stir
nuts and vanilla into the fudge. Then beat with a wooden spoon until fudge loses its sheen,
about 1 minute. Pour into a buttered 8" square pan. Cool and cover pan. When candy is
thoroughly cool, cut into 1" squares. Makes 64 pieces.

** Toasted Walnuts — Spread nuts on a cookie sheet and place in a 250° oven for about 10
minutes. Stir a time or two. Remove from oven and cool before adding to candy. Toasting nuts
for candy recipes does wonders for the candy.*

Herbed Olive Oil

4	fresh rosemary sprigs, or 1 teaspoon dried
6	whole black peppercorns
3	garlic cloves, coarsely chopped
1	Spice Island bay leaf, or 3 others
2	fresh thyme sprigs, or 1/2 teaspoon dried
2	fresh oregano sprigs, or 1/2 teaspoon dried
	good quality olive oil
1	or 2 small dried hot peppers, or 1/2 to 1 teaspoon dried pepper flakes

Place herbs and other seasonings in a clean, sterilized glass quart jar. Add olive oil to nearly fill
the jar.* Cork or seal with a tight lid. Label, date and refrigerate jar. Every day or two, shake
the jar. After a week to 10 days, flavors have developed so oil can now be used. Use within 2
to 2 1/2 weeks. Use in salad dressings, refrigerated marinades, pasta dishes, etc., for great flavor.
Sauté hamburgers or chicken breasts in this seasoned oil. Makes 1 quart.

** Keep herbs and seasonings covered with oil. If allowed to come above the oil line, the fresh herbs
may mold.*

Flavored Oils

Flavored oils have become important "tools" in the kitchen. Like flavored vinegars, flavored oils add tremendous interest to many foods. Oils may be flavored with herbs, garlic, certain vegetables, etc.

Flavored oils cannot and must not be treated like the vinegars. Whereas vinegars have a high acidity, most oils have a low acidity, so the risk of botulism food poisoning is certainly possible in improperly stored oils. Any oil flavored with raw garlic or other vegetables **must** be stored in the refrigerator and then no longer than two to two and a half weeks.

So, when I prepare a flavored oil, I label and date it, and then store it in the refrigerator. I make relatively small amounts at a time, because if it isn't used by the end of two weeks or so, I dispose of it. Don't hesitate to make and give an oil for a gift — just make sure the recipient understands the proper method of storing and using it.

Here are two basic methods of preparing these flavored oils.

1. Ratio is 1 part puréed herb to 1 part oil. Purée the herb (basil, for example) in food processor. Measure puréed herb and add an equal amount of oil to the processor. Blend well. This is a fragile but potent oil. I keep it no longer than a week in the refrigerator. I usually use a nonflavored oil such as corn, soybean, safflower or canola oil for this method. This flavorful oil is wonderful to brush on pizza crusts and to add to pasta dishes. I make only a small amount at a time.

2. This ratio is considerably more oil than herb. I often use an olive oil here, but the unflavored oils are good also. This oil is not as fragile as the one produced in number 1 above, so I keep it for 2 to $2^{1}/_{2}$ weeks in the refrigerator. At left is a wonderful recipe for Herbed Olive Oil.

Ornaments to Paint

*The children will love to help you make these. Set out an assortment of cookie cutters (gingerbread people, star, tree, bell, Santa, reindeer, etc.) and let the children's imaginations take over! By the way, these are ornaments only — they are **not** edible.*

4	cups flour
1	cup salt
1$^1/_2$	cups water

Combine flour and salt. Add water gradually to make a stiff dough. Place dough onto a floured board and knead until dough is smooth and pliable. If it's too sticky, add a little flour. If too dry, add a little water. Once dough is a firm mass, place it in a plastic bag and remove small pieces as you need them. Roll dough to approximately ¼" thick. Cut or form ornaments as desired. Use a nail to put a hole in the top of each ornament. Place each ornament on a cookie sheet and bake at 350° for approximately 30 minutes. Cool thoroughly then paint each ornament as desired — acrylic-based paints are best. After paint is completely dry, you may varnish the ornaments, if desired. Allow to dry completely before threading ribbon or string through the hole. These could become keepsakes if you wrap well and keep in a cool, dark closet until next Christmas. Makes about 1 dozen average-sized ornaments.

11 Spice Chicken Seasonings

Could this be the Colonel's secret recipe of "11 herbs and spices"? Whether it is or isn't, this is a great mix to season chicken. Makes enough seasonings for three chickens.

2	cups flour
$^1/_2$	cup cornmeal
2	teaspoons salt
1	tablespoon dry mustard
1	tablespoon garlic salt
1	tablespoon celery salt
1	tablespoon paprika
1	teaspoon dried thyme
1	teaspoon dried oregano
1	teaspoon pepper
$^1/_2$	to 1 teaspoon ground sage
1	teaspoon ground ginger

Combine all seasonings and store in an airtight container. Add a note to the gift saying: "For one cut-up frying chicken, take out 1 cup of the mixture and place in a heavy paper bag. Shake a few chicken pieces at a time in the bag, coating all sides well. Heat cooking oil in a skillet or frying pan to medium heat. Brown the chicken pieces on all sides. Lay chicken in a baking dish and bake, uncovered, at 350° for about 1 hour."

Great Granola

This is a combination of all my favorite granola recipes. Makes about 14 or 15 cups.

5	cups old fashioned rolled oats (not quick)
1	cup dried apricots, cut into small pieces
1	cup dates, cut into small pieces
1	cup light raisins
1	cup dark raisins
1	cup coconut
1	cup wheat germ
1	cup slivered almonds
1	cup walnuts, coarsely chopped
$^{1}/_{2}$	cup raw sunflower seeds*
$^{1}/_{2}$	cup raw sesame seeds*
$^{1}/_{2}$	teaspoon salt
1	cup corn or soybean oil
$^{2}/_{3}$	cup honey
$^{2}/_{3}$	cup brown sugar, firmly packed
2	teaspoons vanilla

Heat oven to 300°. Combine first 12 ingredients in a large bowl. Set aside. Now combine oil , honey, brown sugar and vanilla in a medium saucepan over medium heat. Stir and heat until well mixed. Pour over ingredients in bowl and mix thoroughly. Grease a 15" x 10" jelly roll pan. Spread mixture in pan and bake for about 45 minutes, stirring every 10 minutes. Cereal should be light brown. Cool thoroughly and store in airtight containers. Give in a pretty glass jar with a ribbon on the top.

* Raw sunflower and sesame seeds are available at health food stores.

7 Beans and 1 Great Soup

This soup is wonderful on a cold day. If you use the turkey sausage, this soup is nearly cholesterol-free. Makes about two quarts of delicious soup.

2 cups mixed dried beans (Select at least 7 varieties from the following list — navy, black, great northern, pinto, red, green split peas, lima, garbanzo, lentils.) Attach this recipe to the jar: "Rinse beans. Place in a large kettle or soup pot. Cover **beans** with water, add **1 tablespoon salt**, and soak in covered kettle overnight. Drain and rinse beans. Add **2 quarts water** and **2 cups diced ham** or **sliced smoked sausage** or **smoked turkey sausage**. Simmer for about 2 to 2$^{1}/_{2}$ hours. Add **1 large chopped onion, 1 clove garlic**, minced, **1 teaspoon chili powder, 1 bay leaf**, $^{1}/_{2}$ **teaspoon pepper**, $^{1}/_{2}$ **teaspoon dried basil** and $^{1}/_{2}$ **teaspoon dried oregano**. Also add **1 (28 ounce) can diced or chopped tomatoes** and **2 tablespoons vinegar or lemon juice**. Simmer for another hour. Taste and add more salt and pepper, if needed."

I have listed some of my favorite sources for flower and herb seeds and plants, potpourri supplies, containers for vinegars, jellies and oils, plus many things the cook and gardener need and shop for.

Burpee's Seeds

300 Park Avenue
Warminster, PA 18991-0001
Telephone: 800-888-1447

Burpee's has quality seeds. I have bought basil seeds from them each year for many years. I also buy one or two of their new seeds of the year — these are listed in the beginning of the catalog. I got my first French vanilla marigold seeds from Burpee's — a beautiful flower to add to an herbal bouquet. I also order giant California tuberous begonia bulbs from Burpee's — the flowers and even the foliage are far superior to the "nonstop" varieties that many greenhouses and nurseries sell.

Shepherd's Garden Seeds

6116 Highway 9
Felton, CA 95018
Telephone: 408-335-6910, Fax: 408-335-2080

The catalog this seed company sends is designed to make you want to try every seed they sell! They give a nice description of the seed and what it produces and even include great recipes. They offer many hard-to-find seeds and European varieties. Their basil collections are superb, especially the Italian Basil Collection.

Nichol's Garden Nursery

1190 North Pacific Highway
Albany, OR 97321-4598
Telephone: 503-928-9280, Fax: 503-967-8406

This is one of my favorite catalogs. The catalog is called *Herbs and Rare Seeds*. Nichol's offers a wide variety of seeds as well as plants, potpourri supplies, and their own blends of seasonings. The herb plants I have ordered from them are well-packaged and ready to go into the ground. Their essential oils (for cooking and for potpourri-making) are some of the best to be found. They also offer many potpourri fixatives that I've had difficulty finding other places. Everything I've ordered from Nichol's has been top quality.

White Flower Farm

Litchfield, CT 06759-0050
Telephone: 203-496-9600, Fax: 203-496-1418

White Flower Farm's catalogs are so beautiful, you'll add them to your coffee table collections! Ask them to send you a copy of their spring catalog and their fall catalog. The plants arrive in perfect condition with very clear and precise planting instructions. Their iris, peony and daylily collections are fabulous. The tulip (and other bulbs) collections are also superb. If you're ever near Litchfield, be sure to visit White Flower Farm and gardens. They carry the Blackmore and Langdon Tuberous Begonia bulbs (commonly referred to as B and L) — the finest and most beautiful begonias in the world (and that isn't just my opinion!). The highlight of my visit to the farm was walking through the B and L greenhouse — wow!

Well Sweep Farm

317 Mt. Bethel Road
Port Murray, NJ 07865
Telephone: 908-852-5390

When you receive Cyrus and Louise Hyde's catalog, you won't believe how many herb plants are available. They offer just about everything — new varieties as well as old varieties that are often difficult to find. This is a very impressive listing from an old established business.

Frontier Cooperative Herbs

3021 78th Street
Norway, IA 52318
Telephone: 319-227-7996, Fax: 319-227-7966

Frontier Herbs is a wholesaler. They have become very important in the herb industry. They offer hundreds of herbs and spices in a most impressive catalog. They also offer more than 100 essential oils, herbal tea mixes, cosmetic oils, and much more. Everything they offer is of superior quality.

Pinetree Garden Seeds

Box 300 - Route 100
New Gloucester, ME 04260
Telephone: 207-926-3400, Fax: 207-926-3886

This catalog is fairly new to me and I'm very pleased with the selection of vegetables, flower and herb seeds they offer. They also offer an extensive list of books ranging from garden calendars to children's gardening books to cookbooks, books on flowers, vegetables, and on and on. The catalog is well-written and concise.

Park Seed

Cokesbury Road, P.O. Box 46
Greenwood, SC 29648-0046
Telephone: 803-223-7333, Fax: 803-941-4206

A beautiful catalog — nearly every seed or plant they sell is photographed in color. Park's has new seeds each year and they are displayed in the front of the catalog. (When I talk about seeds, I mean the resulting plants from those seeds!) You wouldn't go wrong ordering from this company.

Wayside Gardens

1 Garden Lane
Hodges, SC 29695-0001
Telephone: 800-845-1124, Fax: 800-457-9712

This catalog is similar to Park's Seed Catalog. No vegetables, however, but lots of flowers, perennials, roses, trees and more.

Mirsky's, Inc.

P.O. Box 874
Beaverton, OR 97075
Telephone: 800-733-0506, Fax: 503-628-0647

Mirsky's is a wholesaler of very fine quality dried and preserved herbs, flowers, leaves, cones and much more. Their pepperberries are the nicest I have found. The Oregon moss is green and beautiful. The preserved cedar and juniper and even small preserved Christmas trees are all lifelike and beautifully preserved.

The Lebermuth Company, Inc.

P.O. Box 4103
South Bend, IN 46624
Telephone: 800-648-1123, Fax: 219-258-7450

Lebermuth is an old established wholesaler of dried herbs, spices, essential oils and fragrances. The peppermint or spearmint flavoring in your toothpaste or chewing gum may have been supplied by Lebermuth!

Sources *(continued)*

Williams - Sonoma

P.O. Box 7456
San Francisco, CA 94120-7456
Telephone: 800-541-2233, Fax: 415-421-5153

Ask them to send you their catalog called *A Catalog for Cooks*. The catalogs (you'll receive several a year) are loaded with up-to-the-minute cooking tools, pots and pans, small electrical appliances, plus more things than can be mentioned in this short space. They also offer great foods such as special olive oils, vinegars and other seasonings. Just about anything the cook needs for the kitchen can be found in this catalog. If you have a chance to visit one of their stores, do so — the pages of the catalog will come alive for you.

Crate and Barrel

646 N. Michigan Avenue
Chicago, IL 60611
Telephone: 312-787-5900

This is one of my favorite stores! Crate and Barrel has items of excellent quality but at the same time they are reasonably priced. Look for glass herb containers with cork lids, vinegar bottles, inexpensive stemware and interesting pottery in this catalog and store. A great source for Christmas presents.

Index

Index *(continued)*